1 MONTH OF FREE READING

at

www.ForgottenBooks.com

By purchasing this book you are eligible for one month membership to ForgottenBooks.com, giving you unlimited access to our entire collection of over 1,000,000 titles via our web site and mobile apps.

To claim your free month visit:
www.forgottenbooks.com/free286667

* Offer is valid for 45 days from date of purchase. Terms and conditions apply.

ISBN 978-0-265-18814-9
PIBN 10286667

This book is a reproduction of an important historical work. Forgotten Books uses state-of-the-art technology to digitally reconstruct the work, preserving the original format whilst repairing imperfections present in the aged copy. In rare cases, an imperfection in the original, such as a blemish or missing page, may be replicated in our edition. We do, however, repair the vast majority of imperfections successfully; any imperfections that remain are intentionally left to preserve the state of such historical works.

Forgotten Books is a registered trademark of FB &c Ltd.
Copyright © 2018 FB &c Ltd.
FB &c Ltd, Dalton House, 60 Windsor Avenue, London, SW19 2RR.
Company number 08720141. Registered in England and Wales.

For support please visit www.forgottenbooks.com

THE
COMPLETE ATHLETIC TRAINER

THE COMPLETE SERIES

Demy 8vo. Fully Illustrated.

THE COMPLETE ASSOCIATION FOOTBALLER. By B. S. Evers and C. E. Hughes-Davies. 5s. net.

THE COMPLETE ATHLETIC TRAINER. By S. A. Mussábini. 5s. net.

THE COMPLETE BILLIARD PLAYER. By Charles Roberts. 10s. 6d. net.

THE COMPLETE BOXER. By J. G. Bohun Lynch. 5s. net.

THE COMPLETE COOK. By Lilian Whitling. 7s. 6d. net.

THE COMPLETE CRICKETER. By Albert E. Knight. Second Edition. 7s. 6d. net.

THE COMPLETE FOXHUNTER. By Charles Richardson. Second Edition. 12s. 6d. net.

THE COMPLETE GOLFER. By Harry Vardon. Twelfth Edition. 10s. 6d. net.

THE COMPLETE HOCKEY PLAYER. By Eustace E. White. Second Edition. 5s. net.

THE COMPLETE HORSEMAN. By W. Scarth Dixon. 10s. 6d. net.

THE COMPLETE LAWN TENNIS PLAYER. By A. Wallis Myers. Third Edition. 10s. 6d. net.

THE COMPLETE MOTORIST. By A. B. Filson Young. Seventh Edition. 12s. 6d. net.

THE COMPLETE MOUNTAINEER. By George D. Abraham. Second Edition. 15s. net.

THE COMPLETE OARSMAN. By R. C. Lehmann, M.P. 10s 6d. net.

THE COMPLETE PHOTOGRAPHER. By R. Child Bayley. Fourth Edition 10s. 6d. net.

THE COMPLETE RUGBY FOOTBALLER. By D. Gallaher and W. J. Stead. Second Edition. 10s. 6d net.

THE COMPLETE SHOT. By G. T. Teasdale-Buckell. Third Edition. 12s. 6d. net.

THE COMPLETE SWIMMER. By Frank Sachs. 7s. 6d. net.

THE COMPLETE YACHTSMAN. By B. Heckstall-Smith and Captain Ernest du Boulay. Second Edition. 15s. net.

METHUEN & CO., LTD., 36 ESSEX STREET, LONDON, W.C.

THE COMPLETE ATHLETIC TRAINER

BY

S. A. MUSSABINI

IN COLLABORATION WITH CHARLES RANSON

WITH THIRTY ILLUSTRATIONS

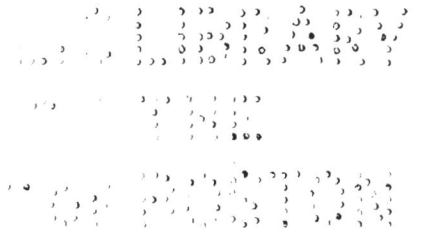

METHUEN & CO. LTD.
36 ESSEX STREET W.C.
LONDON

First Published in 1913

PREFACE

IN the multitude of physical culture counsels derived from all parts of the world, the author believes that none surpass or even equal the old-fashioned English training methods which once stood for our unassailable supremacy in the field of athletics. The American coaches, supposedly gifted with supernatural powers, freely admit that the foundation-stone of their reflected successes in recent years was laid by the teachings of the old school of England's professional athletes. These imply an adherence to simple and therefore natural health rules combined with a nice technical understanding. Nowadays, elementary details are mostly neglected or overlooked, for the reason that most of the qualified track trainers have gone out of business. They and their kind have had to seek other occupations. Some have gone to America, and many are to be found tending to the professional football teams up and down the country. As a result, the willing amateur athletes have lacked competent coaching, and the British Olympic teams have not covered themselves with glory. They have generally been beaten where their predecessors often excelled. The Americans and other competing nations have attempted (and not by any means adopted) professional training on the approved old English lines, especially in regard to track athletics. What shape these lines take it is the purport of this book to illustrate, under the direction of one who has travelled along them. If serving no other good purpose, their production here (and at a time when athletic trainers and training is a topic of the day) may lead to a revival and a better understanding of track and general athletics.

Among all the splendid British field games, the only exception to a generally well-understood set of first principles is to be found in foot-racing. Knowledge is recognised in its highest aspect—that is, as the most powerful agent for progress and improvement—in golf, cricket, football, tennis, bowls and suchlike games of skill. The simplicity of running—and of sprint-running in particular—has seemingly covered up the thousand and one little details to be eradicated or acquired, which go to fashion the first-class and highly polished short-distance runner, such as we met with in the past. In saying so much, there is no attempt to belittle the present-day amateur, nor to suggest that,

PREFACE

given the same understanding of his subject, and the will to put it into practice, he would not do as well or better than the professionals. The natural advantages are on his side; for the old-time professional pedestrian masterpieces came of a class, however strong and hardy, lacking in ordinary comforts and often the bare necessities of life. But they made compensation by their fine technique.

Here is the lesson, then, that I wish to clearly place before the athletes of old England, in the hope of restoring their rather dimmed prestige as the pioneers and most expert demonstrators of the nearly lost art (so far as they are concerned) of track athletics.

In recent times, not only the Americans, but the French, the Germans, the Italians and the Swedes have produced extraordinary runners. It is safe to assert, however, that none of them (except, perhaps, the French) are as rich in raw material as we. Only something stands between us and our regaining possession of the "Blue Riband" of the world's athletics—which, I feel, is more dependent upon the issue of foot-racing than any other branch of sport. This is the somewhat common failure to look below the surface and investigate causes which go to account for there being the usual "wrong way" and "right way."

In regard to the terms and routine of the training here presented, the writer has merely set forth that which would best serve a seasoned professional athlete who could devote all his time and energies to a fairly strict daily routine. This is, of course, impossible to all but the select few.

The average athlete only able to spare an hour or so in the early mornings or evenings will, naturally, take a longer period (and train even more gradually) to prepare himself to arrive at his best state. He is of a class to whom natural physical exercise in the open air means everything—and he should miss no real opportunity of practising either the training exercises (shown in another chapter) or his particular form of athletics.

Boys and youths under twenty years of age (at the least) must be content with much less exacting work until they are grown up to manhood. They only need to practise, without exerting themselves severely, to find style and get a grasp of things. The rest will come later on.

I cheerfully acknowledge the hints and suggestions that I have received from my old friends, Charles Ransom and Harry Perry, in the preparation of this work.

S. A. MUSSABINI

CONTENTS

	PAGE
THE RUDIMENTS OF RUNNING AND WALKING	1
SPRINT-RUNNING	9
200 AND 300 YARDS SPRINTS	54
THE 440 YARDS RACE	59
THE HALF-MILE RACE	66
THE ONE-MILE RACE	70
LONG-DISTANCE RUNNING	76
HOW TO BECOME A MARATHON WINNER	84
TRACK TACTICS	118
TRUE TRAINING METHODS	135
TRACK AND ROAD WALKING	152
THE HURDLES	161
THE LONG JUMP	169
THE HIGH JUMP	173
HOP, STEP AND JUMP	177
PUTTING THE SHOT	181
HAMMER-THROWING	185
SHOES	188
STARTING	195

x COMPLETE ATHLETIC TRAINER

	PAGE
Timing or Watch-Holding	200
Care of the Track	211
Stride Measuring and Tracing	215
Fashioning the Raw Material	221
Training Exercises	223
General Health Hints and Personal Notions	233
Index	263

LIST OF ILLUSTRATIONS

BEAUTIFUL HURDLING . . . *Frontispiece*
    Photograph by J. Woodland Fullwood

	FACING PAGE
RUNNERS AND WALKERS . . .	2
POWER, SUPPLENESS AND PACE .	
A FINE SPECIMEN OF THE HUMAN FRAME SHAPED FOR SWIFT RUNNING	6
SPRINTERS .	18
A SPRINTING LESSON . . .	38

    Photograph by J. Woodland Fullwood

GET SET! 46
    Photograph by J. Woodland Fullwood

THE START FOR THE SPRINT: NEW AND OLD STYLES   52

DIFFERENT DISTANCE TYPES . 60

A BUNCH OF FAULTS . . . 64
    Photograph by J. Woodland Fullwood

ELEGANT MIDDLE-DISTANCE RUNNING: HANS BRAUN, THE GERMAN "QUARTER" AND "HALF-MILER"   68
    Photograph by J. Woodland Fullwood

OXFORD AND CAMBRIDGE MILERS . 70
    Photograph by J. Woodland Fullwood

	FACING PAGE
MILE RUNNERS	74
Photograph by J. Woodland Fullwood	
DISTANCE RUNNING . . .	80
Photograph by J. Woodland Fullwood	
TRACK TACTICS IN RELAY RUNNING .	134
Photograph by J. Woodland Fullwood	
TRUE HEEL AND TOE ACTION	154
A CLASSICAL LONG JUMP .	166
Photograph by J. Woodland Fullwood	
THE ROLL-OVER STYLE OF HIGH JUMP .	174
Photograph by J. Woodland Fullwood	
THE TURN IN THE AIR: A HIGH JUMPER JUST CLEARING THE BAR	176
Photograph by J. Woodland Fullwood	
SWINGING THE HAMMER . .	186
Photograph by J. Woodland Fullwood	

THE COMPLETE ATHLETIC TRAINER

THE RUDIMENTS OF RUNNING AND WALKING

TO fairly appreciate the somewhat lengthy sections of this work which are devoted to foot-racing, it will be as well if the average reader followed the writer's train of thought with regard to the ideal styles of bodily movement. Everybody can run or walk, at a greater or lesser speed, and continue to do so for varying lengths of time—a matter always, of course, dependent upon the individual. To know just how you do your bit of running or walking should be interesting to the average man. It should also induce to a little thought as to what a wonderful creation is the human body. Once this comes to pass, the rest is easy; for anyone of ordinary intelligence will, surely, find entertainment in understanding why it is he runs or walks at will, mostly in an effortless kind of manner, but under " forced draught " when top pressure is applied. If most cannot take sufficient interest in what are truly miraculous powers—each man, woman or child is a living miracle—then one must pause to take breath!

The runner runs and the walker walks out of his nervous energy. His nerves are the governors of his muscles, and these control all other parts. The joints are just hinges encompassed by ligaments and tendons, each shaped to take their especial part in the bending, stretching and in-and-out play. The leg is a long lever which drives the body along by pressure against the ground, rigidly set in walking, but more easily carried in running. *The legs are under the command of the arms, which are equally dominated by the shoulders*, back and chest muscles, in either walking or running. The strain of arm-swing comes upon the upper part of the body and the triceps muscles of the upper arm; the strain of leg-swing falls upon the stomach, loins and groin. The drive comes at the beginning of the stride from the front of the thighs and loin muscles and the push off the ground from the buttocks and all the muscles running up the back of the leg. These are the parts that take the whole weight of the body when the leg is levered up on the toes or the ball of the foot as it is being pushed away from the ground.

The legs are really the instruments of the body, which orders them to its requirements by the agency of the nervous forces. If you closely watch the running of any little boy or girl you will see their arms and bodies loosely but actively engaged in giving assistance to

K. MCARTHUR, WINNER OF STOCKHOLM RATHON NOTE EASY MOVEMENT OF SHOULDERS AND HANDS

A CHAMPION WALKER TRAVELLING AT TOP SPEED
$16\frac{1}{2}$ SECONDS FOR THE 100 YARDS

A SEVENTY-YEAR OLD SPRINTER

THE NATURAL ACTION OF CARRIAGE ARM-SWING AND STRIDING OF A YOUNG MIDDLE-DISTANCE RUNNER

the legs. This is natural movement altogether different to that which we are usually accustomed to view on our running tracks. Now and again some exceptional youngster comes along who does the right thing by instinct, without one in a thousand being able to divine the real reason of his fine running. He only does what others can do if they were made to understand that running is based on a sort of topsy-turveydom, and due equally as much to the play of the transported body as to the swing of the legs themselves.

Nearly every kind of running has its special style, graduating from the flying sprint to the easily taken low paces of the very long-distance track or road work. The poise of the body is more forward at sprinting than at genuine quarter-miling (where the runner goes through with a long, plugging stride). Then the quarter-miler's extra speed calls for a lower carriage of head and shoulders than the half-miler, who, again, should not be quite so erect as the miler. From this stage onwards, however, all are much of a muchness: the running is more flat-footed. But every runner with any pretensions to be at the top of his class should cultivate a turn of speed or sprinting burst, which he can only do if he inclines his head and shoulders more forward than he is accustomed to in the ordinary way of racing, and, getting up on his toes, sets his feet going to a livelier measure.

There is really no form of track athletics so little understood as running and walking. The cross-play of the arms, the right arm lifting the left leg, and the left arm lifting the right leg, should hint at the part that the body muscles have to play in the general effort. Nothing is more certain, too, than that when one is in an unprepared state the stomach and rib muscles feel the strain most acutely. Why, at the opening of a cricket season, or if you are injudicious enough to do some fast or long work on the track after being away from there for some months, and even at bowls or golf, you will get a stiffness and soreness about the ribs which will take some rubbing or wearing off.

Walking—as conducted upon the track—is more punishing than running. The fairer and faster the walker the greater the fatigue. The arms and body swing are his chief concerns. How they help to get the legs along or the rise and fall of the shoulders, the rolling of the hips clearly show. Both running and walking depend chiefly upon the strength and suppleness of the body. The lithe leg, most pliable at the joints, and giving the long drive from the top of the thigh bone to the knee-joint, is their most valuable assistant. A great runner or walker is formed by nature. The critical eye will find him out and linger longingly upon the shapely contour of his figure, the neatly turned joints,

the arched foot, the even distribution of strength; the lissom movements (to be noticed even when he is in his ordinary clothes) of the arms, hips and shoulders, and the quick, alert steps, reveal the athlete.

No two running or walking actions are alike. They may be high or they may be low down to the ground, midway between these extremes with many intermediate variations of either style. The shape of the legs and the play of the hips with their controlling muscles determine the exact nature of the endless mannerisms. For instance, anyone whose leg is above the ordinary length from the knee to the ankle must come up high, while others who are comparatively short there will keep their feet much closer to the ground. But the greatest determining factor of all is the long thigh, flattish at the sides and bulging out on top and behind. That is the sprinting leg; and it is better if the under leg be short: first, because there is not so much to lift; secondly, because the action is bound to be of the creeping, easy kind; and, thirdly, because the swing of the thigh determines the length and speed of the striding. One cannot help running well, given such a leg. But the class in which he will show to best advantage will absolutely depend upon the runner's temperament. The big, quick, restless men must be sprinters; those of less hasty habit will shine at middle distances; and the lightweights at the longer distances, with the ever-present likelihood of an exception popping up in each case to defeat the general rule.

Ordinary running simply means pulling oneself along on the downward leg and by the arms. All move in this manner excepting the true sprinter, whose form of running is a push of the feet, made right under the body, with all the muscles behind the leg and up the back brought into the effort. The correct sprint-runner is quite an artificial product. He uses his arms differently; and the angle at which his head and body should be pitched, to bring him up on his toes and keep his legs well under him, is not possible to be maintained but for the fastest running.

Walking is a draw and a thrust, lacking in the smoothness of both classes of running, the pull and the push. It stands for the finest natural exercise and the easiest mode of progression (away from the track). for the simple reason, that every step means the application of the pull-and-push effort in greater or lesser degree.

The value of track practice, regularly but lightly taken, in the various branches of pedestrianism, is to be found in the gradual development of the needful muscles. Those most in use will draw upon other and less active parts of the body. Thus, by degrees, the legs, the arms, the

A FINE SPECIMEN OF THE HUMAN FRAME SHAPED FOR SWIFT RUNNING

RUNNING AND WALKING

back, loins and shoulders are given their proportionate share of the required power according to how they are employed. This being so, is it not easy to understand that a poor running or walking style will induce to the cultivation of the wrong cords at the expense of others which, really, rank as first in importance? And once a faulty style gets hold of a runner or walker it is only subdued (never fully eradicated) by dint of much striving and a redistribution of strength. In every respect " Habit is second nature."

There is an outcry, at the moment, for novices' scratch races. The idea is commendable. But the best of these young runners should at once be put into the hands of those capable of imparting the correct carriage, arm and foot work for the class of race they have done well in. May the writer be allowed to ask where such tuition is to be found? The multiplicity of false styles to be seen among the best of our athletes (with any approach to the proper technique so very conspicuous by its entire absence) and the coaching instructions he has heard and seen are the cause of his dubious state of mind.

To complete this introduction to the pedestrian section of the book, diagrams of the varying poises of the body for the different running distances and the rigid walking example may not be out of place.

8   COMPLETE ATHLETIC TRAINER

The correct sprinting pose, with the legs operating right under the body.

A sprinter's artificial bounding action.

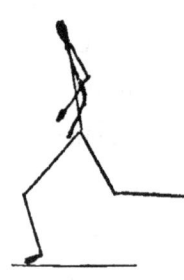

The almost upright position and forward striding of the miler or ordinary track distance-runner.

The erect carriage, lifted arms, straight grounded leg and loose swinging leg of the fast track walker.

The quarter-miler's long-striding and "pulling" action.

RUNNING AND WALKING STYLES

SPRINT-RUNNING

IF there exist any doubts on the ranking of the differing classes of foot-runners, let it be known that the short-distance or sprint-runner stands for the concentrated essence of speed and the acme of vitality. He represents a bundle of compressed energy which expends itself quickly, but in doing so accomplishes the uttermost limits of what the human frame can achieve in the way of locomotion. Fast running is one of the most natural habits with which the physically sound younger folk are endowed. Curiously enough, though, it is the most difficult form of running to acquire so far as track-racing with the indispensable spiked shoes is concerned.

Nature now gives place to specialist doctrines. Even the stride is cut down to artificial dimensions. The runner is schooled to carry himself in what can only be described as an unorthodox style. He has to work at set exercises, in keeping with this department. The old-time sprint coach knew the technique of the business. He was as sure of his methods and as well able to demonstrate and explain them as the rowing, golf, cricket or boxing professional tutors can do.

His apparently meaningless orders and insistence on the carrying-out of minor details, all had a defined purpose in view. And in the fulness of time, dependent, of course, on the good will and obedience shown, the raw material is transformed into an efficient article, the quality of which is now thrown back on its natural resources—that is to say, the degree of aptitude first shown now goes far towards determining the full measures of trained ability.

Not one sprinter in a thousand can run 100 yards through at the increasing rate of speed which he should, and is generally rated to do. He will almost certainly fade away to some extent in the last ten or dozen yards. The faster the runner the more certain is this to be, although a sprinter's " length " extends as far as 150 yards. There will not be that proportionate improvement between the 75 yards mark and the 100 yards that there was at 50 to 75, in contrast with 25 to 50. Only the extraordinarily good finisher (who cannot, however, be a correspondingly fast beginner) will continue to increase his speed throughout the full 100 yards. We have laid stress upon this sprinting feature, because it assists in bringing out a great point, which is clearly unknown or left neglected. This is the need of a sprinter's bodily condition being as perfect as that of the ten-miler, who can more regularly be depended upon to properly stay through his course than the sprinter his 100 yards. Therefore it stands to reason that the one should be as fit as the other, though the training for these widely differing distances are things very much apart. Instances in point can frequently be had in sprint handicaps. The scratch man will often be seen to get right on the shoulders of a middle-marker 20 yards or so from the tape (especially in 120 yards races), and yet be pushed to his uttermost limit to win a few inches or make a bare dead heat, and even yet suffer a defeat. This is evidence that he has not lasted through at top pressure.

In proof of the assertion that few runners can finish out a sprint race, and that it *takes more staying* than any, the following illustrations deserve close inspection. First of all, take the runner who plods on in his own style and gets to do 11 seconds for the 100 yards, he will (in nine cases out of ten) be found to do the first 50 yards in 6 seconds. Therefore, he must do the last 50 yards in 5 seconds, or " even " time, and if going on to 120 yards, he *will certainly get inside 13 seconds*. Now, this class of sprinter is the most dependable of any. His average running is superior for the reason that he is just a little better than the ordinary runner. His strength enables him to go on increasing his speed to the end of the 120 yards. Then compare this gradual improvement with the running of a sprint "flyer" (the 10 seconds for the 100 yards man), who should on the "watch" (which does not mean quite the same thing on the track) give the 11 seconds runner 4 yards in the first 50 yards, and another 6 yards in the next 50 yards.

It will be found on the average of the running in the last 50 yards, that the scratch man is 1 yard 7 inches per second the faster of the two. He *should*, therefore, be able to give away 12 yards 14 inches in the full 120 yards and be on the worsted with our 11 seconds man. But *will* he do so in a race? Look up all the amateur records for years and it will be found that the 10 seconds or $9\frac{4}{5}$ seconds men for the 100 yards have respectively taken 12 or $11\frac{4}{5}$ seconds for the 120 yards. It is clear from this (apart from many ocular demonstrations) that the "even-timers" are no faster than the 11 seconds man, over the last 20 yards. There is a reason for this, as for everything else which happens. The faster the runner, the greater the strain on the whole muscular and nervous system. The effort is so great that he cannot sustain it in a degree proportionate to his pace at 100 yards. His speed is dying away, and the 11 seconds man is now travelling equally as fast. There should, surely, be ample testimony in these comparisons of the sprinter requiring a perfect preparation to increase his stamina.

The technique of sprint-running is a study in itself. Only those who have been through the mill and have ground up the raw material, after separating the husk from the grain, can detail its thousand and one items. This headlong dash through space, when only the fact of your working your legs as fast as they can be driven is known, may almost be said to defy analysis. It has mostly remained so, despite the searchlight of action-photography, because there is no money to be now made by looking closely into its main points. The writer happened to be in the sport at a time when a matter of a few inches often represented many hundred pounds sterling. Where the money is, you get the seekers after facts. First, it was the guiding-line given by the watch, and path and air conditions. Then came the correct form of preparation. Last of all, the search for action-perfection, the most difficult problem of all. Little by little its mysteries were unfolded, mostly out of the mannerisms and styles of the stars of the path. It became plain to understand that each and all had a definite similar aim. The nearer they approached a high standard of ability, the more positive became the reflection of their efforts. The lessons crystallized and set a top-hole mark, such as is established in leading games of skill, of the but slightly varying "right way" and the many variations of the "wrong way." These run all through the long line of athletic sports, from sprint-running to putting the shot.

A low carriage of the hands, the head and shoulders pitched perceptibly but slightly forward, and a tiptoe, bounding gait form the main outline of the good sprint-runner's style. The whole of his anatomy should work loosely and smoothly. His arms are the governors of his legs, and they are propelled by the shoulders. To bring out the best that he is capable of, the shoulders, arms and legs should work in unison on either side of him. So rapid are the movements of the one and the other actuating forces that they are most difficult to follow. Everything is working at tip-top speed. Those looking on are confused at the spectacle, and the correct style is always (or so it would seem) overlooked, and the false, straining type of sprinter the most noticed. None appears to go deeper or to possess the knowledge that the smooth-actioned runner, minus all flourish and bustle, is akin to a sweet-running machine. Mannerisms must not be confounded with a taking style. The art of sprint-running is to produce the maximum of effect by the easiest application of full power. And this the well-schooled sprinter will do.

SPRINT-RUNNING

His pose and body balance, in keeping with the proper placing and working of his arms, and light-footed, true-leg action must conduce to such a result.

"What a fine runner!" The expression is

The sprinting style (front view).

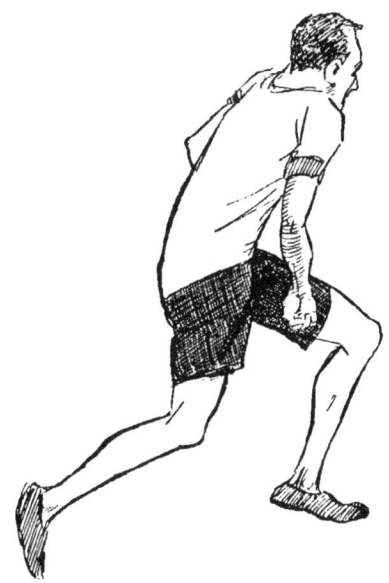

The sprinting style (side view).

quite commonly heard, without there being always justification for it; for the really good runner, especially the sprinter, makes apparently no effort in covering the ground. He is a very near approach to a true-moving piece of machinery. The bad or moderate sprinter's running is all effort—and he shows it. One hears at times of sprinting prodigies who can accomplish all manners of fast times when in an untrained state.

Frankly, they have escaped our own notice. You may get an 11 seconds man at 100 yards, or one slightly faster, and assure yourself that he has the makings of a possible champion. Much will depend upon his shape and build. The greater the scope, the higher the possibility of his development—that is to say, a tall, well-split-up and strongly, cleanly turned youngster will hold physical advantages over one of a shorter, less symmetrically limbed kind, although both may have done about the same time (which implies equal ability) in a preliminary trial. Other than this, the stronger finisher will almost certainly mature into the faster runner. It is safe to assert, however, that if the less-favoured novice be given his running education by a capable man, he will make excellent progress. So, too, will the other ; but unless he is licked into shape by being constantly overlooked until his faults (which every running novice, good, bad or indifferent, possesses) are suppressed, he will only be good where he should be very good, or even of surpassing excellence.

To arrive at the pitch of perfection we should like to see attained by every sprint-runner, the body, arms and shoulders must be strengthened by light dumb-bell and bending and stretching exercises. The ideal sprinter should be a combination of muscular strength, activity, and nervous energy supplemented by his being naturally adapted for fast running. He should preferably be tall, weighty, well split up in the legs (especially from the hip-joint to the knee), neatly turned at the knee and ankle joints, and (preferably) small-footed (in any case light-footed), with a high, strong instep. These are exacting requirements to expect in the one individual runner. Any reasonable selection of them should permit a pretty useful sprinter. But for a real champion top-hole runner, the whole batch of physical qualifications, plus his using them to the best advantage, are absolutely essential. The chief factor in this connexion is an all-round looseness, which can only be developed by the easy, low-lying and across-body motion of the hands.

The hands should be turned inwards, so that the first knuckle-joints face one another; and the arms should swing across the pit of the stomach, the muscles of which will soon be trained to work in accord with the fluent thrust and pull of the arms.

More important, perhaps, than any other detail, is the hitching-up of the shoulders, in their turn, to keep the arms beneath them loosely swung. They work independently, but to the same purpose—namely, to help lift up the flying feet and lighten the effort. A runner who uses his shoulders well, and keeps them bobbing up and down, setting the time to the movements of his arms will never strike the ground heavily. In this way he is bound to skim more easily over it through being more up on his toes than the usual stamp of sprinter, who hits the track hard. From that cause alone he is less prone to a jar or breakdown in the legs. The sprinting ideal is to let as small a portion of the shoe touch the cinders as is possible. To bring this about, the runner must develop the upper half of his body, make it take its share in the work on the approved principles, and be properly shod for the purpose.

The advanced, inclined pose of the head set straight for the tape is the runner's steering gear. Keep it properly placed—that is, looking directly up the track—and you will make a bee-line to the tape. Turn it or screw it aside (as many runners do when they are finishing), and you will more or less interfere with the directness of your course, and the uniformity of your striding. A look over your shoulder will shorten the stride to an almost unbelievable extent. Throw your head back on your shoulders (as, unfortunately, some amateur champions regularly do as soon as they make a supreme effort), and you not only slow your striding, but also add considerably to the strain. As a matter of fact, and to be outspoken, the runners who throw their heads back

A NICE ILLUSTRATION OF THE SPRINTING
ARM AND SHOULDER SWING

A GREAT SPRINTER
IN COURSE OF DEVELOPING THE TRU
SPRINTING ARM, SWING, AND TIP-TO
STEPPING HE IS MOVING AT HIS HIGHES
SPEED

SPRINTERS JUST LEAVING THEIR "HOLES"
THE MORE LEVEL LEG ACTION OF THE RUNNER ON THE EXTREME LEFT IS DUE TO THE
FACT THAT HE STARTED FROM THE STANDING-UP POSITION

on their shoulders act as though they were running the reverse way of the track—in other words, backwards or away from the winning-post. The runner's headpiece is the steering gear of the human speed machine.

In sprint-running (and running of all classes for the matter of that, when practised by the expert) the two feet are mostly and simultaneously off the ground. The movement is a series of bounds from one toe to the other, with the knee-joints first bent and then contracted, as in walking paces. There are two extremes in the way of sprinting actions, either of which may produce, by the process of more or less lengthy culture, extraordinary form. The first of these is the lithe-legged, high-fighting action with knees thrown out in front like an exaggerated copy of a particularly pronounced trotting horse, "throwing them up and out" as the best of his kind will do. There have been very speedy runners, who covered the ground in this showy, eye-taking manner. They are brilliant by comparison with those who simply seem to paddle along with an easy, slinking gait and their feet striking right under them stride by stride. But mere looks do not make the better runner. This low-down-to-the-ground, almost creeping footwork, if not so attractive, has held its own with all other methods. Both extremes present, of course, perfectly natural striding, and bear evidence to the law that no two men are built or run exactly alike. The half-way house of running actions is represented by the common conception of how leg movement operates. It is the commonplace run adopted by most of us, with the knee neither kept low nor lifted too high, and the steps taken neither under nor much in advance of the body. Altogether, this medium in the way of running styles is good to see, and if never quite responsible for phenomenal achievements, it has not lacked first-class demonstrators of its merits.

A stride of 7 feet 6 inches may be considered the full sprinting length even for very tall men when they are running their fastest (as nearly all will be found to do) from 40 to 100 yards. They are at the very height of their speed within these limits, with leg-drive at its snappiest and best. But 7 feet 6 inches is only for the very long-thighed sprinter. The majority will be found to cover between 6 feet (the other extreme) and 7 feet. Extraordinary cases of runners over six feet in height not striding more than 6 feet, and yet showing brilliant speed, have been known (notably that of George Wallace, of Thornley, a professional sprint champion of the seventies, who could do 6 yards inside "evens" at 130 yards). The sprinting stride needs to be shorter and, of course, more quickly taken than at any other distance.

A very interesting feature of sprint-running (more than any other form) is the liability, nay probability, of a runner who is trying to give away more start than he can do or is up against a better man, literally going all to pieces and running considerably slower than he usually does through trying too hard. When he finds he cannot gain or is losing ground, there are very few runners who will not struggle all they know in a sprint. If they are gaining, or cannot see their opponent, all is well. They run in the usual way. It is when they can see him, however, that in their desperate efforts to catch or hold men who are running away, holding their lead or passing them, they strive too energetically, and, "losing their shape," do fail to even show their proper speed. A nice test case in point is this: say two runners, one receiving a yard start in 100 yards, won a dead heat. At the second time up give the start-receiver another half-yard start, and see what happens! Receiving an equal start in either race, the start-receiver will not improbably win by all or nearly all his start.

You will at times have heard of a jump for the worsted at the finish of a race and the wonderful things which have been so accomplished.

Some extraordinary effects have possibly occurred in this manner. But there are few sprinters of real ability who could break the machine-like action of their legs to attempt such a performance. A jump means changing the feet or taking a momentary pull to gather yourself together for a flight of this kind. No gain will really be found over the usual long-striding finisher with the head and chest thrown as far forward as possible in the last stride. The clever sprinter—that is, the trained man of proper deportment—is not poised for jumping, nor should he be. If you run to a point well beyond the winning-posts you will go through them as fast as your legs can carry you.

The proper use of corks means carrying them loosely in the hands until the moments of a starting or finishing effort. Then they are gripped tightly. To a sprinter their assistance may mean half-a-yard gain in the last twenty yards, and they help to keep him together in "shape" during this straining period.

On the Track

To come to something positive, let us go out upon the track. The first things the old hand will take into account are the directions of the wind and the state of the path. If there is no weather-cock, try watching the direction taken by the smoke from the neighbouring chimneys or the play of a flapping flag. Should neither be in view, holding up a handkerchief or throwing up some scraps of paper will show the play and even the force of the breeze. Having discovered the quarter it comes from, during a stroll round of a couple of laps or so in ordinary walking costume, the runner is well advised to have the wind as much as possible at his back during his sprint. The condition of the cinder path will better reveal itself by the prints of his spikes than in any other way. Firm, fast going shows a clean impress and the path otherwise barely disturbed. By contrast, a dry, crumbling or wet, soft path will pull out badly or be so near the consistency of a pudding as to cause the runner to turn his feet sideways for the purpose of ensuring a grip. Either defect means loss of time, but the pulling-out fault is nothing like so speed-lowering as the very soft, yielding stuff. The limit of this is reached when the sun melts the overnight frost to turn everything underfoot, cinder path or turf, into a boggy, sticky miniature morass. The other extreme is the frost-bound, ridgy track (which may easily cause a breakdown), whereon you can never get your balance or a proper foothold. A second on to one's ordinary time at 100 yards can easily happen under such circumstances.

Having seen to the conditions, the trainer goes to the dressing-room and directs the runner to use his short, medium or long spiked shoes, according to his impression of the path being either hard, good-going, or soft. If the weather is cold, he counsels the wearing of long under drawers and a sweater. Letting the runner warm up his circulation with some brisk dashes, he then scoops out his holes and gives him two or three cracks from the pistol at 40 and 50 yards. There is an interval of a few minutes between each spin, in which the runner saunters back to his holes. While he is doing so the critical trainer will be closely examining the imprints of the runner's spikes, and even measuring his strides. Their trail should tell him much of what he wants to know, whether they come in a straight line and the runner's feet uniformly find the same places (as they should do), and also something of the speed he is getting up (judged by the shortness or length of the paces). This examination of the footmarks on the track can hold up a veritable mirror to the observant trainer or runner.

So surely as improvement comes, or the runner trains off (as he will do if he is under weight, or overworked or out of sorts), the fact will be set forth upon the track. The footprints will tell what has happened. By his extra dash, which means quickened action, the runner will get in another stride or two, if he has a wind behind him, or the path is firm and fast, or he is feeling particularly well in himself. This extra stride or strides means quickened movement, like the additional beat of a watch or added revolution of a wheel. On the other hand, with the wind against him, on a dead or loose track, or when below par in himself, the uneven stride or strides will again show where deficiencies of pace and time have occurred. The reason of stride-measuring which tells to a nicety how many strides the sprinter averages to take in covering his distance, when he is running well, should be understood from this. But whereas a gain is shown by extra striding, a loss is mostly represented by irregular and crooked footmarks.

The work finishes up with the stride-through and the top-speed burst for the last 30 or 40 yards of the 150 taken. Here again the trainer's eyes should never leave the runner, and any symptom of getting the arms or head up or perceptible struggling should be the signal to turn off the pressure. Top speed should be turned on at a given mark on the track, and the spot where the runner held out signals of distress, shown by his losing his proper pose, should be noted. He must keep pegging away at the distance in his stride-through and finishing dashes until he can pass it comfortably, and go right on in correct shape.

To prove to a runner the defects which accompany his getting " out of shape," take him over his tracks and show him his shortened stride and altered footmarks. They will be there plain enough to see, and he will know out of his own feelings that he was straining and tiring where he had just previously been travelling smoothly and freely.

The Sprint-Runner's Preparation

Three months, or thirteen weeks, is not too long a period of training for the sprinter. The first four weeks should be devoted to easy preliminary work, for the purpose of strengthening the legs and body to their full task. Quite gentle spins on the track up and down the straight, and some occasional slow laps and nice swinging walks in the neighbouring country, with never a thought of fast running, is the programme for this first month. Only get out of the holes quite slowly and gradually work up to half and three-quarter speed. Then, at the end of a fortnight or so, three-quarter speed, while avoiding all idea of a trial or racing against anyone. You are just getting your muscles

SPRINT-RUNNING

into shape and strengthening them to the more serious work ahead.

Right at the beginning of the training, the most important detail is the care of the feet, and the toe-nails in particular. Keep them trimmed short, and hollow the big toe-nails out at the top in this fashion ⌒ . Be careful not to cut into the quick. The reason for cutting the nails in this manner is to prevent them from growing into the sides of the toes. The painful inflammation so often set up is thereby avoided. Purgative medicine, which will touch the liver as well as the stomach, should be taken at the outset and for the first few days and at every week-end. A very good old-fashioned recipe known as "Black Jack" will not easily be bettered. It takes the form of $\frac{1}{4}$ lb. Epsom salts, 2 ozs. each of bar liquorice, gentian root, camomile flowers, and a little powdered ginger. Place in 2 quarts of water and boil down to 1 quart. Strain through muslin or a fine sieve, and bottle off, adding a little alcoholic spirit (preferably rum or gin) for preservation purposes. Take a large wine-glassful on an empty stomach at night or in the early morning.

All the stiffness and pains which the runner is sure to feel at the beginning of his training should be relieved by hand-rubbing to the feet and legs. An occasional warm bath also helps to soothe and soften them. The back muscles of the thigh, the calves and the big tendon which runs up the leg at the back of the ankle (known as the Achilles tendon) will be sure to feel sore at different times. The act of getting well up on his toes will put an unaccustomed strain on these points of the runner's legs, which they will not easily adapt themselves to. Among the chief causes of breakdowns or strains is taking pistol practice before your early stiffness has gone, or you have warmed yourself up with some preliminary trotting about the track; or by the change from a soft to a hard path; from an uneven track; or by pulling up too sharply when travelling at top speed. And when a sprinter breaks down he is not easily patched up again. Those who believe that a runner who has burst or ruptured the sheath of a thigh muscle (the commonest form of breakdown) can be put right in two or three days have a greater faith in human nature, as represented by the athletic trainer, than the many unfortunates who have had some first-hand acquaintance of such mishaps. Rest is the only real remedy for a breakdown, and very easy work the cure for stiffness or slight strains.

Only very gentle spins each morning and

afternoon must be taken until all feelings of stiffness have departed. Up to this time, runs of 40 to 60 yards at nice half-speed will represent the work upon the track. Be sure not to commence too quickly, and, above all, *do not pull up too suddenly. Let your legs go moving on and gradually slow down to a walk.* While taking these pipe-opening runs—and three or four each time you turn out, and a trot round the whole lap to finish up with—you must try to cultivate a good style of carriage and tiptoe footwork. A good pair of shoes will help in this.

The golden secret of getting the very best out of a sprinter that he is capable of at both ends, beginning and finish (the middle part will then take care of itself), is to practise out of the holes and gradually lengthen the top-speed burst at the end of the stride-through. The finished sprinter should go like a piece of clockwork from the report of the pistol right through the worsted. He should stride in the same place every time; and he will do so if he is thoroughly wound up. In this way, he will not deviate even a bare few inches in two races run at an interval of twenty minutes or so, when running against the same opponent each time. Weather fluctuations will, of course, affect the times on the watch. Learning to begin is a much simpler matter than acquiring a strong finish, which must be developed by degrees during the fast sprint winding up the stride-through. Make a mark on the track where this should begin, and keep increasing the length of it 10 yards at a time, until you can master a full 100 yards.

There is nothing more unsatisfactory than a loose, ill-fitting pair of running pumps. When, as is mostly the case, they have the spikes badly placed for the runner's tread, then he is indeed in trouble. If the spikes do not stand straight out from the sole, and are leaning away towards the sides of it, here is proof positive that they are incorrectly set for the runner's tread. And he will not be comfortable nor capable of doing his running in them until the heads are shifted in between the soles in answer to the runner's proper requirements. A loose shoe is an annoyance at all times. On the other hand, you cannot have too tight a fit. A really good pair of sprinting shoes should fit as tight as the tightest pair of kid gloves, be rounded rather than square-toed, and take equally as much getting on. They should be of non-stretching leather, too, so as to retain their shape as long as possible. There is as much as a couple of yards' difference to the sprinter (and the better he is the more does it tell!) between a good, tight-fitting pair of pumps set with spikes just where they come under his tread and a loose pair with the spikes incorrectly placed. The nearest comparison that can be made is to be found in the buoyancy of a fully blown-up tyre or india-rubber ball and the flabby inertness of the same articles when they are "down." To ensure a good fit, it is absolutely necessary to be specially measured by a practical man. If you have a pair of old shoes you have been wearing they will be of service in telling the shoemaker where the tread is and, of course, the proper positions for the spikes.

A very bad fault, common to most amateur sprinters, is walking about the track on tiptoe. There is nothing so binding to the calf muscles. These should be, like all other parts of the legs, nicely pliable. Walking flat-footed in between the spins will be found a great relief from the strain of getting up on the toes while running.

The sprinter in training must be careful to avoid other pastimes or exercises than those which are needed for quickness and the using of all the body muscles. Cricket, bowls, football, any effort, in fact, which calls for one-sided strain, must be avoided. If the effort is not equally distributed all over the body, stiffness and soreness is sure to result; and the sprinter with aching muscles and sinews is of no account. Walking on greasy, slippery, frozen or snowed ground will often have such a bad effect upon his legs as to throw him back several yards. These matters will be detrimental to all classes of runners, but trebly so to the highly tuned-up sprinter, and especially if he is of the very pronounced leggy type.

After four weeks of preliminary practice, when it will be found advantageous to be out on the track at the hour which the race you are training for will be run, and, therefore, get you to adjust your meal-times accordingly, you should then be strong and well enough in all respects to undertake some serious training. Now you have built yourself up (nearly every sprinter will go up in weight during this easy first month) the trainer will try to keep you to your increased poundage, while putting you through a stiff and serious course of exercise, morning and afternoon (Sundays excepted), in the second month. Now the pistol practice and sharp bursts-out of the holes at 30, 40, 50 and 60 yards, with an occasional top-speed dash right through the 100 yards, and a regular striding finishing burst of 200 to 250 yards. Run this at nice three-quarter speed, striding out freely and letting yourself out all you know for the last 50 yards. Remember to maintain a good style: hitching the shoulders in time to the swing of the lowly carried hands across the pit of the stomach, keeping the head and body pitched nicely forward, and getting well up on your toes. The moment you feel your arms are going up, slow off. Never get your hands or your head up; keep yourself in nice, compact shape. To struggle is to at once lose speed and cultivate bad habits.

Plenty of 40 and 50 yards dashes out of the hole, sometimes from a slow beginning, at others putting " all in " to the crack of the pistol, will begin to sharpen you up. Take your time between each of these, so that you are breathing normally before you have another run out. If you can get the company of other sprinters in these short dashes, which should always be run to a line of worsted or mark placed on the track, they will help to stretch you out. The faster they are, the better for you. Put your heart into your work and do everything very seriously. Make up your mind that you are going to improve, and leave nothing undone that will assist towards this end. This middle five weeks of your training is really the most critical of the three months. The benefits of the hard work you are now doing will be felt later on. After a fortnight of this keen running practice a full-dress rehearsal of the race, as represented by a trial over the full distance, can be attempted. The trainer will already, no doubt, have made a pretty shrewd guess at the pace of his charge in the course of these few right-through bursts which have already been taken. But now the ordeal is a more exciting one, it will have been so long looked forward to, apart from the influence it should have upon the actual race. The first trial is a mighty serious business to all concerned, and to the runner more than anyone else.

If the training is taking place during the winter-time, or there is a desire to make little use of the runner in these special tests, the services of a dependable "trial-horse" or understudy will be found of the utmost value. The varying weather conditions of winter-time in England often baffle the most expert judgment as to their effect upon the checkings of the watch. So, to get the line of form and gain a knowledge of what the "going" is like, another runner is requisitioned. He needs to be reliable, rather than fast. The 11 seconds for the 100 yards man is just about as good as can be got for the purpose. He is the "happy medium" among sprinters, the natural runner who will vary very little one week with another. But whatever his pace, the chief requirement of your "trial-horse" is consistency, so that he can tell the watch-holders how comparatively slow or how fast the day is, and also race in the trials with the man who is being specially trained. The dependable trial-

SPRINT-RUNNING

horse" is invaluable. To keep a careful watch over his progress, as there is always the possibility, if not the probability, of his either training on, or training off, the "trial-horse" should very frequently be run against the watch.

Walking, but not too much of it, is beneficial to sprint-runners. A nice swing of the arms across the body and striding out freely from the hip, while keeping every part loose and alive, is the best style to adopt. Set the pace at about 4 miles an hour and be satisfied with a nice bustling 2 to 3 miles at this gait. A sharp walk of this comparatively short distance on Sundays, and two or three times a week, is better than a long, slow trudge. It will be quite far enough for most sprint-runners. Only those unfortunates who put on flesh quickly, and have to keep their weight down, need to do more daily walking than this. For sprinting, when one is getting to the top of form, plenty of rest and lying about (preferably in the open air) is the chief consideration. A stroll of a couple of laps around the track before and after your spins will suffice for most runners. This and an easy mile or two's-walk before breakfast, and again in the evening, should comprise a day's work. The scales will tell you nearly all that is needed about the runner's well-being and progress.

It is in the last of the three training months

that the really trying period arrives, when the runner (or the trainer, or both) become "fed up," or steeped in anxiety as to the outcome of it all. With his system now strung up to a very high pitch of tension, and feeling as though he could "tear up the track," and have a race "right through" his distance every time he turns out, the runner needs very careful handling. According to his temperament, he may be obstinate, cheerful and willing, or bored to the verge of distraction. The trainer's task is now to try and keep his man in as happy a frame of mind as circumstances will permit; to create confidence in his ability to win; and, above all, to prevent him doing too much work upon the track. When the high-water mark of "condition" is reached, the work must be of a lighter description, with the runner remaining as strictly regular in his habits. When it is made clear by trials (which should only be few, and fairly far apart) that the runner has come to his best, or made such improvement as befits his task, he should be eased off gradually in his work. One crack from the pistol, and some half-speed, quick footwork, and the canter through with a finishing dash at the last 40 yards (not more) will keep him tuned-up and in good order. By daily checking his weight and carefully supervising his habits, he can be kept in first-class trim. The least signs of

SPRINT-RUNNING

staleness, overwork or a cold mean his being rested and given some additional flesh-forming liquids, such as good stout, or milk in fairly liberal quantities. A cold or chill must be cured before training is resumed. Staleness or overwork will wear off when the normal standard of weight is again reached.

When a sprint-runner is in the best physical trim, he never seems to be satisfied with what he can do. He is so fit that his energies are never seriously taxed. The better he gets, the less he feels the effort of going through, say, 120 yards, or 300 yards for the matter of that, at the top of his speed. When he was only half fit, however, another and a very different tale had to be told. It was very hard and very distressing work then, with a decidedly slower time returned on the watch. Now it is easy and a pleasure to do. That is where the danger of doing too much lies. It is far better to do too little than too much, saving yourself for the race. Repress the strong inclination you are bound to feel to have more than one top-speed burst of 40 to 50 yards, and the quick " pattering." The great idea is to go to the mark for your race, absolutely bursting to have a full-speed dash as the result of having done little or no fast running, although regularly exercising your legs for several days previously. Be, preferably, a " bit above yourself," a pound or two heavier than your normal weight. It will be nothing against your running nor the state of your nerves.

It may sound as something of a fad, but the fact remains that many a comparatively poor finisher at 100 or 120 yards has derived the utmost benefit from a run (not on his toes, but just on the pad of the foot) in his ordinary clothes and boots before breakfast. Starting with 250 yards, and getting used to this, the distance is lengthened to 440 or even 500 yards. The pace is quite a half-speed one—that is to say, at the rate of 10 miles per hour—which would, of course, mean the 440 yards being covered in about $1\frac{1}{2}$ minutes. Strengthening the body all over and stimulating the breathing organs, this exercise, which may be taken on the roads or paths, has transformed not a few runners, who could not maintain their sprint dash right through, into fairly powerful finishers.

As a guide to the varying classes of sprint-runners a schedule of times is set out over some intermediate distances of a 120 yards sprint, which should be closely studied and tested. It does not pretend to actually present the actual times of the runners as they pass the different points, but they certainly will do so approximately and to within a yard or so. But the difficulty of getting rigid standards lies in the

A SPRINTING LESSON

SHOWING HOW THE SCRATCH MAN (IN THE FURTHER STRING) LOSES A RACE THAT HE SHOULD HAVE WON BY FLINCHING AT THE TAPE AND RAISING HIS HANDS

SPRINT-RUNNING

fact of no one running through on quite an even keel of gradually increasing pace. Some are relatively faster at 50 yards, others do their best running from 50 to 90, and, again, the exceptional sprinter is far better in the last 50 than the first; and so on according to the peculiarities of each individual. But this schedule does give, in its true colours, the average of the running and its full result in the wide bounds which divide the championship class from the lowly 12 seconds man for the full 100 yards.

Schedule of Average Times made by the Various Classes of Sprint-Runners at 120 Yards

	50 yds.	75 yds.	100 yds.	120 yds.
The 12 secs. man	$6\frac{2}{5}$ secs.	$9\frac{1}{10}$ secs.	12 secs.	$14\frac{1}{4}$ secs.
,, $11\frac{3}{4}$,, ,,	$6\frac{3}{10}$,,	$8\frac{9}{10}$,,	$11\frac{3}{4}$,,	$13\frac{9}{10}$,,
,, $11\frac{1}{2}$,, ,,	$6\frac{1}{5}$,,	$8\frac{4}{5}$,,	$11\frac{1}{2}$,,	$13\frac{3}{5}$,,
,, $11\frac{1}{4}$,, ,,	$6\frac{1}{10}$,,	$8\frac{3}{5}$,,	$11\frac{1}{4}$,,	$13\frac{1}{4}$,,
,, 11 ,, ,, (The average sprint-runner)	6 ,,	$8\frac{1}{2}$,,	11 ,,	$12\frac{9}{10}$,,
The $10\frac{3}{4}$ secs. man	$5\frac{9}{10}$,,	$8\frac{3}{10}$,,	$10\frac{3}{4}$,,	$12\frac{6}{10}$,,
,, $10\frac{1}{2}$,, ,,	$5\frac{4}{5}$,,	$8\frac{1}{10}$,,	$10\frac{1}{2}$,,	$12\frac{3}{10}$,,
,, $10\frac{1}{4}$,, ,,	$5\frac{7}{10}$,,	$7\frac{9}{10}$,,	$10\frac{1}{4}$,,	12 ,,
,, 10 ,, ,,	$5\frac{3}{5}$,,	$7\frac{7}{10}$,,	10 ,,	$11\frac{7}{10}$,,
The "inside evens" prodigies	$\begin{cases}5\frac{1}{3} \text{ to}\\ 5\frac{1}{4} \text{ secs.}\end{cases}$	$7\frac{1}{2}$,,	$9\frac{3}{5}$ to $9\frac{1}{5}$ secs.	$11\frac{4}{10}$ to $9\frac{1}{8}$ secs.

There you have what is reasonably the whole gamut of sprinting classes. Interesting contrasts may be made of the beginning speeds when it is pointed out that $1\frac{3}{4}$ seconds is quite fast time for the first 10 yards, and that an $11\frac{1}{4}$ seconds man (for the 100 yards) should do "even time" (that is, 20 yards in 2 seconds) from the 100 to 120.

There is no attempt made to glorify the sprinting giants of the past beyond their real worth. They were all quite as good as the bottom figures on the schedule made them out to be ; and most of their training and racing performances took place in mid-winter, when the air and paths slowed the times to an almost incredible extent. It is not an exaggeration to allow from $\frac{1}{5}$th to $\frac{1}{4}$th of a second at 120 yards for the retarding effect upon a sprinter as the difference between a fine winter's day and general summer conditions. The warmer, lighter air and firmer track found in the months of June (occasionally), July, August and September mean much to the time of a runner. Those are the days for records. If sprinters like Hutchens, Gent and the like had had a favourable midsummer shot at record 10 yards inside even time (at 120 to 130 yards) would have easily been credited to them.

The "Crouch" v. the "Stand-Up."

Without the ability to quickly "leave the mark," or make a fast beginning, there

SPRINT-RUNNING 41

is no hope for anyone to become a champion sprinter. Natural aptitude in this direction does not necessarily imply coming greatness. As a matter of fact, the raw fast beginner, who gets away full of fire and dash and is "in his running," or regular striding, within the smallest possible lapse of time, never holds out the promise of improvement which the experienced eye can trace in the novice who does the best of his running during the second part of the race. It has been proved times out of number that a runner may be taught to begin well, but with very few exceptions can he be improved in anything like a corresponding degree at the finish. A quick beginning is more or less a knack. It depends upon the runner being "set" in an advantageous attitude. The smaller or medium-sized men will, usually, be quicker on their feet —they have less weight to move than the big, upstanding runners. But mark this—and mark it well—when you do get the big man quick on his feet, he may not unlikely turn out a world-beater, a champion of champions. The old sporting adage that "a good big 'un will beat a good little 'un"—and as we might add, middle-sized 'un—holds true to-day as when first expressed.

The old English style of standing up while awaiting the crack of a pistol (and under which style we developed such a school of sprint-runners as found no equals in America and Australia) has given place to the crouching-on-all-fours importation.

The crouching-down style has been responsible for more bad and unfair starting than the average lover of athletics may be induced to give credit to. Just because some foreign sprinters came over here and made some fast times and displayed abnormal speed " off the mark," it was taken for granted that their style was the most serviceable. "Getting a move on the gun" (as the Americans have it), or "beating the pistol" (as we used to know it here in England), was made simple. By putting his hands beyond the allotted mark and moving forward at the call of "set" (an almost imperceptible movement known as body pressure) the practised runner could depend upon getting the better of the start over any but the most expert of pistol-firers. If nicely on the go forward, his advantage could be estimated in yards.

A certain Transatlantic scratch runner could be relied upon to "get the pistol" three times out of four. He was a comparatively small man, yet he looked a sprint phenomenon up to 60 or 70 yards, by giving useful sprinters 2, 3 and 4 yards in the first 20 yards of the journey, only to fade away and barely last the "hundred"

SPRINT-RUNNING 43

through. This runner was glorified as a sprint marvel—and so he was as far as anticipating the start was concerned. If he bent too far forward he used to diplomatically fall down on his hands, and the firer waited until he reset himself and had another shot at the "intelligent anticipation" business. All the crouchers-down were partial to it. But with a tried hand fingering the fire-arm, the practice is dangerous. Should he fire when the croucher has pressed forward as far as his body can go, then it means being "left" at the start. The "crouch" has certainly not contributed towards fair starting, and the huddled-up poses of the men on the mark are not so easily distinguished in the act of being "on the go," as in the pre-crouch days, when the runners stood up clear to see.

Now to the technique of starting. As explained, there are two extremes in the way of positions or stances for the start—namely, crouching-down and standing-up, with many detracting variations of the proper way in either. For the present crouching-down fashion, the runner makes two holes well behind his starting-marks, one for each foot at graduating lengths, and he gets down on all fours by leaning forward on the tips of the fingers of both hands. It will be found on trying this position that the body has a certain play. If, at the starter's signal call of "set," to warn the runners he is about to fire, and despatch them on their journey, a stealthy forward motion of the body is made, there is no doubt about the increased speed at which he leaves his mark. His body is under way before the pistol sounds, a circumstance adding considerably to his initial pace. Some foreign runners we have in mind studied the habits of a pistol-firer (even going so far as to time the interval between the call of " set " and the crack of the pistol), and were mostly successful in taking a spontaneous bob forward just as the firer's finger pressed the trigger. Result—a " flyer " (a flying start which is by no means a stranger to the best regulated of crack amateur athletic meetings) and the race rendered farcically unfair. Whether it be believed or not, we say emphatically—and not without a long and close intimacy with our subject—that the only reasons which can be urged in favour of the crouching-down start is its ability to induce a " flyer " for the good practitioner, and a steady stand for the novice and bad stander. Only those who do not know will deny the fact that the Olympic sprint at the Shepherd's Bush Stadium held as glaring an example of the unfair application of the crouching-down position as could well be applied. The Americans appreciated the situation, and it did not tend to soften

SPRINT-RUNNING 45

their feelings when a bigger incident went against them. This by the way, however.

It is safe to assert, simply because it is true, that the line of sprinting champions which we could point to in the days of the old Sheffield Handicaps—Hutchens, Wallace, Jackson, Petley, Shaw, Gibson (of Mordan), Gent, etc.—all stood up to the start. And they stood still as statues, *because they knew that they had a pistol-firer behind them.* Standing up as they did, their bodies were in clear perspective to the starter's eyes. Taught to poise themselves on the mark at about the same forward pitch as when in their running, they took no risks of anticipating the pistol. They did not make mistakes, therefore, but were certain time after time to leave their marks at a regular rate of speed. They were never left, and they never tried to " beat the pistol," as they knew the practice to be a dangerous and uncertain one. Let this clearly be understood, too, that in their day, twenty-five to thirty years ago, there were real sprinting flyers. At least a score of standers-up could run their first 50 yards in $5\frac{1}{2}$ seconds, while the top-notchers stood between this time and $5\frac{1}{4}$ seconds. These last figures accredited to and (without doubt) accomplished by two men who stood up at the start.

The great drawback with the rank and file of

amateur sprinters in the pre-crouching-down days was their woeful ignorance of the proper way to stand. To watch an amateur sprint handicap in those times was to see the majority of the competitors swaying about or falling down on their hands and getting over the mark. Their inability to stand steady had not a little to do with the wholesale acceptance of the crouching-on-all-fours style, apart from its (then) allowing them to put their hands beyond their marks. Yet, had they taken a little pains, and observed the attitude of the steady standers-up, it would have come home to them how much more comfortable and assured is the erect posture as compared with the cramped and tiring crouch.

I am thorough in the support of the old-fashioned standing-up stance at the start, both as regards effectiveness and fairness.

A glance at the accompanying illustrations (on page 52) will show the stand-up stance at the call of "set!" It needs only one hole, that for the back foot. The front foot is put crosswise and planted flatly and firmly, from heel to toe, down to take the whole weight of the body. The distance from the toe of the back foot (which is also placed crosswise in the hole) to the heel of the front foot is about 2 feet, dependent to a very few inches either way on the runner's length of leg. Whatever this be, it should leave

GET SET!

SIX OF THE BEST KNOWN LONDON SPRINTERS ON THE MARK (SHOWING GOOD AND BAD POSITIONS)

SPRINT-RUNNING

him easily but very steadily posed. The body and head are pitched forward at about the same inclination as when he is running. The arms are set in the manner which will best give them a good starting impetus, to get the shoulders and legs and hips in spontaneous motion. The right arm is shoulder-high and almost directly behind the left arm low down, but not close to the body ; the knees are bent, and the whole pose (as may be seen) is one of nice, supple alertness, easy to maintain and comparatively untiring.

There are essential differences between the processes of the two styles. Both have their weight pitched forward and the knees bent. But, whereas the croucher takes part of the strain on his upper arm and shoulders, although it still remains mainly centred on the stomach, back, and the thigh of the front leg, the stander-up throws the whole pressure on to his advanced leg. In both instances, the back leg is held loose and limber in its hole.

The first movement of the croucher is to raise his arms and give a swing of the back leg. Being hunched up on all-fours to begin with, the croucher cannot get into his running with anything like the celerity nor smoothness which was a characteristic of the stander-up, who goes straight as a die from his one hole. The croucher starts from an unnatural, forced position which prevents him getting those " fly wheels " of human motion (the arms) into immediate play; the other is (or should be) nearly in his correct running attitude from the outset. If the scientific analyst were to turn his mind to the problem of which is the most desirable and, therefore, effective style (apart from the faster running the standing-up start has undoubtedly been responsible for), there would be some surprises in store for those who are such out-and-out supporters of the " crouch."

In most matters there is no line of form to be had between exponents of past generations and these of the moment. Fortunately, however, track athletics provide one of the few exceptions. The watch (and many of the same watches are being held to-day as were held thirty years ago !) tells us that the standing-up starters, were mostly faster beginners than the best who have been seen since the crouch came into vogue. And they were stronger and faster finishers, because their stand was not so much of a strain. The very nature of running, which implies instantaneous, independent action of the shoulders, arms and legs, stands in support of the old-time style.

The one leading action needful in the stand-up start is a first short, forward movement of the front foot, technically known as the " dab."

SPRINT-RUNNING

This sets everything (back leg, either arm and every part of the runner) moving. It is a loose-limbed but hustling effort to work up speed. The practised runner will appear to dash straight away into his running with low and stealthy but most swiftly taken strides which soon attain the normal length.

I have many times heard the respective merits of the old-fashioned and new-fashioned starting stances discussed and heatedly argued upon, without there being sufficient proof furnished either way to justify the contentions set up by the opposing sections. About the most "mixed metaphor" criticism, emanating from one, who is not without belief that all he delivers himself of is authoritative, I have heard was this: "The crouch gains a runner half-a-yard at the start, but the stand-up start gains him half-a-yard at the finish." Now, what is one to make of this statement? A gain of half-a-yard at the starting end of a race means a multiplication of the distance in short sprints, where initial velocity means so much. If either stance gives a starting gain it certainly will do so all through the race.

Viewed in a purely mechanical light, any comparison of the two styles is entirely in favour of the old-fashioned stand-up. While the "croucher" sets in a most contracted, tiring position, the stander-up (who knows his business) is at his ease. It little matters to the good stander whether he is kept a few seconds more or less on the mark. If it comes to that he can *stand on one leg and still keep his balance* far longer than the croucher can tighten himself up for his spring. Get a back view of two experts (not a couple of novices nor an expert and a novice) in either style and note the smoothness of action, directness and quick manner of getting up full steam by the stander-up, and the rather strained movements of the croucher. Then trace their footprints and judge (if you will) which is the easier style, which gets the runner the more rapidly into his regular stride, and which calls for the expenditure of the most energy!

For the big, heavy runners, the stand-up—the correct stand-up—is far and away the best starting method. They have not to lift their weight to anything like the same extent as with the "crouch." They can, and should, stand in the attitude that they will run with arms free. It is just a matter of a little coaching (by a capable man), which will be worth all the time expended over it. The fastest beginners were the old-time sprinting cracks, who kept their stance very much of a close secret among themselves. The writer happened to be rather exceptional "out of the hole," and a close student of how the champions did such wonderfully fast 50 yards running. This was really the secret of their truly remarkable speed all through, for no man unable to cover the first 50 yards in about $5\frac{1}{2}$ seconds can hope to do any really fast running at any of the short sprint distances, which range up to 130 yards.

Without a doubt, the best style in respect of the crouch is to be found in putting all the weight and pressure possible upon the arms and hands. At the report of the pistol a pull at the track with the fingers, bringing the hands smartly backwards and upwards, with the idea of getting the loose back leg into immediate action, will put the runner in position and on his legs as quickly as can be done.

The lower he can comfortably keep to the ground with his knees (as he takes his footholds in the holes) while setting on the mark the faster will he get away. Much will depend upon how he makes his holes and the distance these are apart. Every runner should find his proper length—that is to say, the distance between the holes and how near the front one can come to the starting-line. Ease and freedom is the thing to aim for.

Making the right sort of holes is another matter over which you cannot be too careful.

The back hole should be dug nearly straight at the rear and slightly scooped away forward to allow the foot to come easily out. The front hole, on the other hand, should be slanting to give room for the ball of the foot to easily rest upon. A most vital detail of the start is to come quite straight out of the holes with either foot. It should be constantly practised.

A sprinter cannot be too careful about the "holes." Always try them with a run out or two and see that they are firm; for if they give way ever so slightly when you put full pressure on them in the race, they will, most likely, rob you of any chance of winning.

Confirmed habits are most difficult to eradicate in runners, and it would not be wise to try to change the starting style of a seasoned runner. But for novices, and the bigger they are the more favourable it will be to them, there is much virtue in the standing-up style of starting —whatever people who blindly follow in the steps of a prevailing fashion may think.

The photographs of the two starting positions, the old-fashioned and the modern, will further reveal that the croucher has to give the stander-up a nice, useful bit of start and quite enough for him to win a race by. Note the positions of the feet in either case and the way that the stander's head and body are pitched well in

A START IN THE NEW AND OLD STYLES

THE IDEAL CROUCHING POSE OF THAT SPLENDID LITTLE SPRINTER, W. R. APPLEGARTH

AN OLD-FASHIONED STANDER-UP CHARLES RANSOM (A DUAL SHEFFIELD HANDICAP WINNER, WHO HAS RUN HIS 50 YARDS IN $5\frac{1}{4}$ SECS.) NOTE THE FRONT FOOT AGAINST THE LINE AND THE OVERHANGING POISE OF HEAD AND CHEST

A FRONT VIEW OF THE STANDER-UP ON THE MARK

THE START FOR THE SPRINT NEW AND OLD STYLES

SPRINT-RUNNING 53

front of the starting-mark. And a good stander-up can maintain if not add to this advantage from an equally good croucher. This is not mere blind partisanship, but a knowledgable judgment passed upon a subject which has been carefully weighed in the balance.

The real reason for the "crouch" taking root in this country was the original advantage it afforded of the runner being allowed to place his hands and body beyond the mark against which he set his front foot. Now that this has rightly been ruled unfair, and made illegal, the croucher is handicapped by having to finger the starting-line.

200 AND 300 YARDS SPRINTS

THE preliminary preparation for these long sprinting races does not differ in any respect from that of the short sprints. After a quiet three or four weeks spent in strengthening the legs, arms and body by the easy indoor and track exercise detailed at the end of this chapter, longer and stronger bursts may be taken—a full five weeks of pistol practice (preferably twice daily, morning and afternoon) at 30, 40 and 50 yards, finishing up with a nice half-speed stride-through for 120 yards. Full speed is turned on at the 100 yards mark. The distance of this finishing burst should be lengthened 10 yards—that is, from 20 to 30, 30 to 40, and so on until the runner can go quite strongly and in the proper form (and the one thing goes hand-in-hand with the other), until the 200 yards mark is reached. In the last month 50 yards bursts from the pistol and the stride-through (dependent upon the state of the weather, and the feelings of the runner), not forgetting to put all in in the last 50 yards. The chief concern, however, is to keep the arms down, the head and body at a nice forward poise, and get up on the toes. One needs to be strong and well to control all these items when running at top speed.

Some good brisk walks, the dumb-bell and skipping-rope exercises, and a regular course of living are needed to keep one up to the razor-edge of condition for these long sprints. A close scrutiny of the bodily weight, and an easing-off of very severe work, the last two or three days before the race, must never be overlooked. One of the most remarkable characteristics of these 220 and 300 yards, which are ostensibly a greater physical tax than the short sprints, is the ability many poor finishers at 100 and 120 yards have shown in them. In fact, not a few have proved comparatively better at 300 yards than the shorter distance. The reason for this can be given. Having arrived at the top of their speed at 80 yards (as so many runners do), they have dropped into a long, plugging, yet quick, stride, and been able to carry it through the long length of the 300 yards. The real—that is, very quick-striding—sprinter will need to be very strong to go rattling through this course without a very appreciable depreciation of pace.

Some big strong men, who are slow starters and do not get fairly into their running until they have gone some 30 or 40 yards, and have no chance in first-class company at the short sprints (although they will come with a rare rush in the last 20 yards of a 120 yards race), will go very strongly through a 220, and better, relatively, at 300 yards. Runners of this exceptional stamp will probably run the second 100 yards faster than the first. But the ordinary sprinter will show a falling-off at the 220, which is correspondingly increased among all classes of runners at the longer journey of 300 yards. Thus, a $10\frac{1}{2}$ seconds man at 100 yards, although he takes a flying start at the second 100, is unlikely to do 21 seconds for the 200 yards, unless he be a surpassingly powerful finisher. Then, again, at 300 yards his pace will have so dropped that he will be hard put to it to get through in $32\frac{1}{2}$ seconds.

There should be no waiting or dallying in a 220 yards race (now almost generally run in stringed tracks), but there is a certain scope left to the clever runner in a 300 yards. On the customary quarter-mile track, it means the negotiation of two corners. There may be plenty of trouble to the possibly bunched-together top and middle-mark competitors before the straight is reached. As a rule, however, the extreme backmarkers have a pull by being out of the scrimmages (along with the actual leader), and are able to get an unhampered passage into that tiring, long finishing straight.

200 AND 300 YARDS SPRINT

The 300 yards is no end of a gruelling race to the unfit or half-fit runner. But the right type, the strong, lusty young men, find it just nicely within their sprinting powers—when they are fit. There is a distinct falling-off with the best of them, however, in the second half of the 300 yards. Up to about 150 yards the speed is fairly well maintained. It is greatest, however, with nine out of every ten between 70 and 130 yards. Thereafter comes the decline, made more acute in the last 80 yards than anywhere else. The speed is dying out, the feet are now longer on the ground and less in the air than they were. The average rate of progress per second is slowing down right until the runners rush through the winning-posts.

How great a sprinter old Harry Hutchens (the most brilliant of all time) must have been, to have run (as he undoubtedly did do) his 300 yards in 30 seconds, moving around a large field of widely strung-out long-start men on a holding path and getting in front 50 yards from the worsted just "paddled" through, with barely moving arms (not dropping his hands, as the usual expression has it, because he always *kept them down*), at his leisure. This freak among sprint-runners was undoubtedly good for 29 seconds, if he had cared to specially train for the distance (which he never did do).

It is difficult, in mentioning the subject of 300 yards running, to omit the name of the greatest of them all, who (however the statement may be out of place) was, moreover, equally the master of all sprint-runners (past or present) from 60 yards to as far as he liked to run. There is no doubt about this!

AVERAGE SCHEDULE OF LONG SPRINT TIMES

	100 yds.	150 yds.	200 yds.	220 yds.	300 yds.
The average good runners .	11 secs.	$16\frac{1}{2}$ secs.	$22\frac{2}{5}$ secs.	$24\frac{4}{5}$ secs.	$34\frac{1}{2}$ secs.
The $10\frac{1}{2}$ seconds sprinter . .	$10\frac{1}{2}$,,	$15\frac{3}{5}$,,	$21\frac{2}{5}$,,	$23\frac{3}{5}$,,	$32\frac{1}{2}$,,
The 10 seconds sprinter . .	10 ,,	$14\frac{4}{5}$,,	20 ,,	$22\frac{1}{5}$,,	$31\frac{1}{5}$,,

THE 440 YARDS RACE

OF all distances, this is popularly supposed to be the most trying. To the partially trained runner, who is most likely merely a sprinter, it is all this. But the strong, long-striding, well-trained man will go bang through the worsted at the end of a quarter-mile race and take some 30 or 40 yards to pull up, in proof that he could have gone on considerably farther had he been required to do so. The fact of the matter is, the quarter-mile is not in the sprinting class, which practically closes at 300 yards. It comes in the category of middle distances. In proof, you get the real quarter-miler able to get the half-mile and 1000 yards. Long, free striding is the chief requisite at all these distances.

At the quarter-mile, the powerful, long-limbed middle and heavyweights are the ideal men over the course. They taper away in weight, however, at the half-mile, but the length of leg should still be there. The true stamp of the quarter-miler is one who can go all the way through at top pressure. He is not fast enough— that is to say, not sufficiently nippy on his feet in the first 100 yards—to hold his own with the good sprinters. His time over 100 yards would be somewhere between $10\frac{1}{2}$ and $10\frac{4}{5}$ seconds. His pace will be found to come with long striding, and not the quick action of the good sprinter. These comments may be taken as a hint to many who have stuck to sprinting, and who have never got out of the second class, to try the quarter-mile. But they would be unwise if much under the average height of 5 feet 8 inches, and strongly knit. To the first-class sprinter, however, there is nothing more likely to take the fine edge off his speed than a term of quarter-mile training. Once this has left him it will not easily, if ever, be recovered.

There are two ways of running a quarter-mile. They depend entirely upon the type of runner. The very strong runner, short of that bit of extra dash which makes the top-hole sprinter what he is, can go plugging all the way through. He may not find a position on the "inside" of the track to begin with and have to go round one or two of his rivals. But he will be coming to his own end of the race in the last 100 yards. That is one way of quarter-miling. The other presents a more direct course round to the winning-posts. But it is only open to the fast, lively actioned

A FINE SPECIMEN OF THE BIG, UP-STANDING SPRINTER. NOTE THE CLEAN-CUT AND LENGTH OF LEGS

THE TRUE TYPE OF THE POWERFUL, LONG-STRIDING QUARTER-MILER

THE LOWLY, EASILY CARRIED ARMS OF THE GOOD DISTANCE RUNNER

DIFFERENT DISTANCE TYPES

THE 440 YARDS RACE 61

stamp of runner, who is, in reality, a sprinter. His speed will carry him to the front, and he should see that it does do so by getting away from his holes with the pistol crack. For about 80 yards he should continue his top pace. Then, nicely in front, as he should be, and master of the track, he can ease off the full strain by reaching out more and striding rather longer at about three-quarter speed. His quick sprinting action and the effort to maintain it will both have now disappeared. The impetus of his first dash will help to keep him moving at a smart pace. Sticking close to the inside, practically waiting in front and allowing no one to head him, our sprinting quarter-miler can keep up his free, long striding until about 120 yards from home. Here he should gradually gather himself together and never make the mistake of trying to make a final sprint without having taken this precaution. Having set his head and body, arms and legs in the correct sprinting pose, then he can make his all-out dash down the finishing straight. To this kind of runner, who has more speed than stamina, the quarter-mile is a hard race indeed.

Since the Olympic games became fashionable, two distinct types of quarter-mile races have come into existence. The old style, with an open track for all, demands racing craft and experience, and an advantage to he who possesses that extra turn of speed which will get him in the first flight, preferably with the lead, at the outset. The new style introduced in the London and Stockholm Olympiads, with a separate stringed-out path for each runner, if more difficult to gauge, does not make the same demand upon track generalship, nor lend itself to the usual vicissitudes so often arising from a mixed field racing at and on the bends. Its only requirement is judgment of pace. The usual quarter-mile race means a sprint for the first corner and a wise disinclination to resign the leading places by those who have secured them. With equal wisdom, the runners in the rear would be well advised to save their efforts until the finishing straight is reached. Mostly, it is a waste of precious energy, time and distance to make an earlier bid for the leadership anywhere else when you are racing against runners of your own standard. Above all, never try to pass an opponent on a bend. If you are able to do so there, what can you not do with him in a straight?

The Quarter-Miler's Preparation

The cultivation of speed is the first requisite, on exactly the same lines as the sprinter, whose

THE 440 YARDS RACE 63

training should be followed out to the very letter. The only difference is the need of plenty of good, brisk walking and longer track work by the quarter-miler. He takes the clearing physic and the other preliminary attentions. His is also a thirteen weeks' training. Out on the track twice a day, Sundays excepted, he is to all intents and purposes undertaking an identical, only a stronger, preparation to that of the sprinter. Again, the first three or four weeks are devoted to gentle half to three-quarter speed exercises around and about the track, to strengthen the wind, body and limbs. Exercises with dumb-bells and skipping-rope will again assist in this. After the fourth week of the training, the hard, serious work begins. Pistol practice out of the holes at 40 and 50 yards, and the stride-through to finish with. This and the extra walking form the only contrast to the work of the sprinter. A stride-through at good half-speed up to 150 yards and a top-speed 25 yards to finish with, which should be lengthened 25 yards at a time, until the runner masters a finishing 200 yards. This carries him, of course, to 350 yards, which may be considered the limit of the training spins.

Only now and again should the full 440 yards be covered, and then only for the purpose of a trial, say three or four times within the last six or seven weeks of the training. The great idea is to train for speed as against distance. Remember the old adage: "It's not the miles you travel but the pace that kills." If you can dash through 200 yards at the end of a striding half-speed 150 yards and feel fit and well (as a well-trained runner should do) there will be no doubt about your staying the full 440 yards, and probably a good bit farther. The chief thing is to keep in good form and carry yourself with a nice, swinging gait, in most particulars corresponding to the deportment of the sprinter. A good, hard middle five weeks with daily walks of 4 and 5 miles at about $4\frac{1}{2}$ miles an hour, striding out freely from the hips and well swinging the shoulders and arms, will furnish the necessary stamina.

The big, heavy men who are inclined to put on weight will benefit with a good walking sweat once a week. In flannels and sweaters they should be taken along at a nice, free gait until in a glowing perspiration. Then the cool-down, the bath and rub-down, as laid down in the training section.

[TABLE HERE

A BUNCH OF FAULTS

BEAUTIFUL HURDLING

THE 440 YARDS RACE

Quarter-Mile Times Schedule[1]

	100 yds.	200 yds.	300 yds.	440 yds.
The "average" useful quarter-miler . .	12 secs.	$23\frac{4}{5}$ secs.	$35\frac{3}{5}$ secs.	53 secs.
The 52 seconds man	$11\frac{3}{4}$,,	$23\frac{2}{5}$,,	35 ,,	52 ,,
The 51 ,, ,,	$11\frac{1}{2}$,,	23 ,,	$34\frac{1}{2}$,,	51 ,,
The 50 ,, ,,	$11\frac{1}{4}$,,	$22\frac{2}{5}$,,	34 ,,	50 ,,
The 49 ,, ,,	11 ,,	22 ,,	$33\frac{2}{5}$,,	49 ,,
The $48\frac{1}{2}$,, ,,	$10\frac{3}{4}$,,	$21\frac{3}{5}$,,	$32\frac{4}{5}$,,	$48\frac{1}{2}$,,

[1] *Note that these times represent the* AVERAGE *running at the intermediate distances, a fact which does not imply that they exactly represent each individual case, although the final results will be the same.*

THE HALF-MILE RACE

AGAIN at this distance, as in the sprints and quarter-mile, the breathing organs, the heart and limbs must be gradually accustomed to stand the strain of a searching training. Thus, the first four weeks of a thirteen weeks' preparation are devoted to cleansing the system, gentle half to three-quarter speed runs, the introduction to the clean, regular living, which is the mainspring of the whole process. Good brisk runs from 100 to 200 yards, and walks of 3, 4 and 5 miles, and a run-through at half-speed from 300 yards to a quarter of a mile, will gradually tune the runner up until he is fit to stand some fast work. He should keep to runs of 200 and 300 yards, carried out at a nice, free, striding pace. Then finishing up each set of track exercises with a stride-through at good half-speed for 300 yards, at the end of which a good three-quarter speed burst should be gradually extended, until 500 to 600 yards is mastered. As in the quarter-mile (and any middle distance or distance preparations) the full course should seldom be covered, except for an occasional trial.

THE HALF-MILE RACE

There is no race where judgment of pace in the first half of the distance counts for more than in this 880 yards. It is simply fatal to any chance of success, no matter how good the runner may be, to run the first 440 yards much, if anything, under a minute. As a matter of fact, the man who can do this and have enough left in him to get through the second 440 yards without falling quite dead licked on the " tape " should do about 1 minute 57 seconds for the full half-mile, a rate of travelling that few can reach in England, where the atmospherical conditions are, generally, inimical to fast times. It will be noticed by this time example that the runner has gained 3 seconds during the second half of the journey on his 1 minute for the first half of it. The more one analyses the pace at which the first 440 yards of a half-mile should be run and a rigid time-schedule set, the clearer does it become that a 3 seconds' deficiency in the first lap (as compared with the full distance proportionate rate) will be found to suit all classes of half-milers, including the plugger, who delights to go all the way.

It is well known that a good quarter-miler—say a 50 seconds man—if he increases his stride-through and final burst to half-mile requirements, could be transformed into an excellent half-miler. This is providing that he keeps to about 1 minute for the first 440 yards. He will be well advised to try 62, 61, 60, 59½ and 59 seconds, and the watch, in combination with his feelings at about 700 yards or so, will tell him all he wants to know.

Plenty of good sharp walks of 4 to 5 miles an hour, dumb-bell, skipping and punching the ball, or "bell fighting," will assist in bringing one up to a fine pitch of physical condition. As in all other cases, the middle five weeks of the training should be the most severe; the weight and temperature checked at every run or walk. The last three or four weeks will be of a less exacting kind, with a gradual easing-off of hard work as the day of the races comes on.

Cultivation of a turn of sprinting speed is to be had by top-speed 200 to 300 yards about twice a week after the first month of slow work. The carriage of the half-miler is a little more upright than that of the sprinter, but he should carry his arms low and generally assume a loose, easy pose and use his shoulders to assist in the swing of the body. For a final sprint, the runner should gather himself together, and the increased pace must first come from the more rapid play of the arms (still held loose and low) across the body, which must now, with the head, be inclined farther forward than during the slower-taken and longer normal half-mile stride.

ELEGANT MIDDLE DISTANCE RUNNING HANS BRAUN, THE GERMAN "QUARTER" AND "HALF" MILER

NOTE THE BOUNDING STRIDE RIGHT ON THE BALL OF THE FOOT, THE FORWARD PITCH OF HEAD AND BODY, AND THE EASY CARRIAGE OF THE ARMS

Half-Mile Times Schedule

	440 yds.	660 yds.	880 yds.
The good average half-miler	1 min. 7 secs.	1 min. 35½ secs.	2 mins. 4 secs.
The 2 mins. man	1 ,, 3 ,,	1 ,, 31⅗ ,,	2 ,, 0 ,,
The 1′ 59″ ,,	1 ,, 2 ,,	1 ,, 30⅘ ,,	1 ,, 59 ,,
The 1′ 58″ ,,	1 ,, 1 ,,	1 ,, 29⅗ ,,	1 ,, 58 ,,
The 1′ 57″ ,,	1 ,, 0 ,,	1 ,, 28⅘ ,,	1 ,, 57 ,,
The 1′ 56″ ,,	59 ,,	1 ,, 27 ,,	1 ,, 56 ,,
The 1′ 55″ ,,	58 ,,	1 ,, 26⅕ ,,	1 ,, 55 ,,
The 1′ 53½″ ,,	57 ,,	1 ,, 25 ,,	1 ,, 53½ ,,

THE ONE-MILE RACE

THERE have been many and various types of good mile runners, from the short and stocky or lithe and sinewy kind up to the ideal of the tall and far-striding, of whom W. G. George and A. N. S. Jackson stand as the most illustrious of past and present examples. A first-class standard of 4 minutes 20 seconds for the mile appears to correspond intimately with $10\frac{1}{5}$ seconds for the 100 yards 50 seconds for the quarter-mile, and 1 minute 57 seconds for the half-mile. To get inside these times implies marked ability. The miler who can beat 4 minutes 20 seconds, no matter how favourable the day and track may be to the performance, is in a very select class.

Big, medium-sized and comparatively little men have accomplished this fast performance, and the best of the bunch, such as George, Cummings, Snook, Tincler, Bacon and A. N. S. Jackson (not improbably the equal of any) have made really remarkable times for the intermediate quarter, half and three-quarter stages. The great mile-runner will be found to be quite a useful sprinter, a much more

OXFORD AND CAMBRIDGE MILERS

A. N. S. JACKSON, THE CELEBRATED OXONIAN IS LYING THIRD BEHIND HIS PACEMAKERS

THE ONE-MILE RACE 71

than average quarter-miler, very little behind championship form at the half-mile and as good as can be met at three-quarters of a mile. He is, moreover, capable of running 10 miles and more and be a champion all the time.

The mile is an exacting race, for which the regular thirteen weeks' preparation will be found teeming with sound regular work after a quiet three or four weeks' opening. No long distances at first, but gentle daily half-speed runs and nice, striding walks. Gradually tune up the organs inside and out on the lines laid down for the shorter distances. Do not do any tiring work on the track or road, nor in respect of the indispensable dumb-bell, skipping, ball-punching or bell-fighting exercises. As the inevitable soreness and stiffness wears off, which it is bound to do after some three to four weeks regular practice twice a day, runs of 800, 900, 1000, 1100 and 1200 yards can be covered. The state of the weather and the feelings of the runner should be the guide as to the distance.

As in all other cases, train to develop speed. A fast quarter and a good pelting half-mile taken on alternate days and sandwiched in the usual free striding runs will be found of great help. Maintain a real good pace as far as possible. Plenty of long, swinging walks will help to give the required stamina. By such means a good half-miler may be made a good miler. The difference again lies, as between the quarter-miler and half-miler, in longer and stronger work.

Stride-measuring and tracing the footprints should (as in sprinting) be regularly pursued. These matters will often reveal, in company with the scales, the cause of any loss of speed (as shown on the watch). It is when the strides are irregular and crooked that something is wrong with the runner. Every deviation from the regular line of his course means a loss of ground, which multiplies tremendously in distance races.

There are robust milers who will require long sweats and much severe running and walking to get them to their best. On the other hand, there are the natural runners, to whom very little training, just an occasional half-mile, 1000 yards or three-quarter mile, say every other day, and then at nothing like " all out " racing pace, is all that is needed. These are the most difficult kind to train and understand. They are light and dainty eaters, as a rule. The best policy is to humour them and let them have their own way, while keeping very strict note of their weight and general health. As at every other distance, a pound or two on the heavy side, so long as the runner feels well

THE ONE-MILE RACE

and is doing a reasonable amount of training and living regularly, is an advantage.

A miler should run his race at a nice, even pace. He should have experimented to find out what will suit him best for the quarter, half and three-quarter distances, leaving him strong enough to keep going through the last quarter-

A miler.

mile. A tip-topper will usually run a very fast first quarter, very little outside a minute, and gradually lose on this more and more through each of the next three-quarters. This is miling of the best sort, disdaining the waiting tactics which so many adopt, and thereby making their first and last quarters faster than the middle two.

For a handicap race with its many runners,

backmarkers and those with starts of a more or less extended degree alike, the first-mentioned all-the-way tactics are almost inevitable. You must go after the leaders and be up in the first flight as early as can be, at a pace, however, that will enable you to last out the full distance. The scratch runners have the added task to their already difficult one of conceding start. They have to catch and pass the runners interposing between themselves and the leaders. And it is necessary to be within striking distance, if not right up among them, when the bell rings for the last lap. In a level race the waiting game, trailing off the willing pacemakers, or, better still, setting a nice easy gait ahead of the field, and leaving it in the lurch at the last lap, is the usual thing. This is where you are most likely to get the fast first and last quarters, and a slower two middle quarters. Handicap races and level races are things apart, and where the one is usually an all-the-way affair, the other lends itself to the method of the patient tactician, who should be able to turn on more than a passable burst of speed at the given moment.

A high authority on this particular branch of running (none other than the record-holder, W. G. George) lays it down that the third quarter of a mile race is far and away the most trying of the four. There is no doubt about this being

MILE RUNNERS

ILLUSTRATING A MODERATELY GOOD BATCH IN THIS CLASS, WITH THEIR DIFFERING STYLES

correct. A third quarter is the crisis of the race, especially when all have started on level terms. It is here where they begin to closely watch in expectation of a dash from someone or another. There is a sort of calm, even though each runner is anxiously intent on the real struggle to come. The feelings are strained, and the ringing of the bell for the final circuit comes as a relief to all concerned. This third quarter finds out the moral qualities of the runners and their racing craft.

One-Mile Times Schedule

	¼ Mile	½ Mile	¾ Mile	
The 5 mins. man	68 secs.	2 mins. 25 secs.	3 mins. 42 secs.	5 mins.
The average useful miler	65 ,,	2 ,, 18 ,,	3 ,, 31 ,,	4 mins. 45 secs.
The 4′ 30″ man	62 ,,	2 ,, 10½ ,,	3 ,, 20 ,,	4 ,, 30 ,,
The 4′ 25″ ,,	61 ,,	2 ,, 8 ,,	3 ,, 16 ,,	4 ,, 25 ,,
The 4′ 20″ ,,	60 ,,	2 ,, 6 ,,	3 ,, 12½ ,,	4 ,, 20 ,,
The 4′ 16″ ,,	59 ,,	2 ,, 4 ,,	3 ,, 9½ ,,	4 ,, 16 ,,
W. G. George's great 4′ 12¾″ world's record.	58½ ,,	2 ,, 2 ,,	3 ,, 7¾ ,,	4 ,, 12¾ ,,

LONG-DISTANCE RUNNING

THE real miler can run a good 4 miles, and the four-miler can generally stay through 10 miles, and there should be no limit to the distance that the ten-miler can traverse. In all cases it is a matter of training, and the pace set. The mistake of running the full distance, except once in a way as a trial and an experience, should never be made. All along the line it is a matter of developing speed as against running the journey. For instance, for a 4 miles race, runs of $1\frac{1}{2}$ to 2 miles, following the term of easy preliminary work, taken at a good rousing pace, will benefit the runner infinitely more than to keep pegging away at the full course. As a matter of fact, some champion ten-milers have never gone beyond this distance, and mainly prepared themselves for the effort by long, fast walks. This is, however, going to extremes. The ten-miler should, at least, make a practice of taking occasionally 5 mile spins and then (but less frequently still) of 6, 7 and 8 miles, with one full-course trial.

A man who can run 10 miles can accustom himself to double the distance. From that stage there is nothing to prevent his going 50 miles, at the reduced pace this longer journey calls for.

The two great matters to be taken into account are: firstly, first-class physical condition brought about by a long and gradual preparation, and a well-arranged time schedule to set the pace. Long, swinging walks, not strolls, starting at 2 and 3 miles and working upwards, by degrees, to 15, 20 and 25 miles, and runs of a like distance, always at a faster pace than that of the actual race is ever likely to be, will equip the miler for a 50 miles run.

Again the truthful adage, " It's not the miles but the pace that kills," must be given prominence. Care of the feet, the careful cleansing of the system, plain, nourishing food, regular habits and a fresh-air living with daily practice on the track or road-walking, and bending and stretching, dumb-bell, skipping, and the other exercises detailed in another part of the book, must be adhered to. In all cases, see to a change of clothes, wearing the lightest texture (outside and inside) to suit the season of the year. Be sure that your boots and shoes fit you well, not too large, nor too small, and that they are a nice width across and at the toes.

For the very long distances a pair of light spats or thin, tight-fitting socks, strung with elastic at the tops, will be found serviceable, in **dry**, dusty weather, as a preventative of grit getting inside and chafing the feet. If the shoes are made with the seams lapped over and sewn outside, further security against foot trouble will have been gained, as often enough a rough inner sewing and seam have been known to set up painful friction. A long-distance runner cannot have his task made too comfortable for him.

Perhaps the most needful quality for these protracted runs is determination. It may come of stubborn or light-hearted natures, to be equally valuable in either case. The runner who can keep plugging away through a 10 miles grind on the track has a sense of responsibility, apart from his physical attainments, which many may envy. Across country the changing scenes and circumstances relieve the monotony that besets the track runner.

On a very long journey, light, sustaining food and drink, such as concentrated beef tea, milk or barley water, may be given (in small quantities) with advantage to runners. On no account give them stimulants, except, perhaps, in the very last stages of their task. In ninety-nine cases out of a hundred, however, nothing more reviving than being hit on the nape of the neck with a sponge saturated in the coldest obtainable water, and then squeezed over the head, can be had. Change his shirt if, as is likely, it is badly

LONG-DISTANCE RUNNING

wetted. A pailful thrown over a collapsed runner will rouse him like nothing else can do. The very smallest measure of liquid, or other internal refreshment as possible for the physically fit man (and none other should attempt a long journey), who may really not need anything more than to rinse his mouth out and gargle his throat, is another vital point.

Next to the matter of temperament comes the question of style or carriage. A very good distance-runner, who should know better, has laid it down that the movement of the arms should not be across the body. He says that *the arms should be carried at the sides, and be moved up and down.* This is rather staggering intelligence, emanating from such a quarter. As one led to believe that Nature dictates all that is simplest and best in the matter of easy, enduring bodily motion, the writer is opposed to such teachings. The arm-action which comes most natural to the distance-runner should usually suit him best, and will further be in accordance with his striding.

A distance-runner's easy and rather upright carriage.

A close observation of the running methods of

young children show that only a very small percentage of them fail to move the hands (which are loosely closed) in a circular manner across the stomach. The few who do not quite get their hands there still work them slightly inwards and outwards, but, curiously enough, mostly with opened palms.

The famous Finn, Kohlemainen (the hero of the Stockholm Olympiad), belongs to this class, which provides the exception to a very good rule. There is the inward and outward swing of the arms, as the opposite legs are, respectively, raised or dropped, but in nothing like the same noticeable manner as when the hands keep rolling across the stomach, as in the more common styles.

It is the same, too, with the youths and young men when they first take to the running track. Their natural arm-action is smooth and quite unforced. But as soon as they try to run faster or farther than they are accustomed to do, up go their arms, their bodies and heads go up with them, and their stride is strained and retarded. Others cultivate windmill, or see-sawing, or stiff, taut poses (with a false notion of attractive carriage), which keep the shoulders rigid and set, instead of swinging in beat to the swaying of the hips at the strides.

The old-time professionals hung their arms down with the hands loosely set on their corks,

DISTANCE RUNNING

at about groin level, just as one walks in the streets. Theirs was cultivated arm-work, however. It was easy, not showy, and well fitted to the work. But one cannot say that it improved

A boy's natural run (arms swinging across the body).

The unnatural—arms-at-the-sides beating up and down.

upon Nature's carriage across the stomach, which so many great runners have adopted.

Now, with all due respect to those who advocate the rigid carrying of the arms at the sides, the writer wishes it to be known and understood that, for the vast majority, no more stilted arm-play, detrimental to stride, shoulder and hip rolling, could well be conceived. The position it forces upon the average runner is unsuitable. Nothing assists a distance-runner more than getting a gentle, swinging roll, which up-and-down beats of the arms simply prevent. To give emphasis to this matter, the accompanying sketches of a boy's natural, loose play of the whole body, head, shoulders, arms and legs, can be compared with the stiff poise of a runner carrying his arms at his sides and using them with up-and-down strokes.

It is necessary to drive these matters as far home as may be done by letterpress and illustrations, for the reason that at least one trainer at the principal London grounds has been seen (by the writer) to advise his charges to run with their arms at their sides, and chop up and down from the elbow. Nothing more painfully ugly and unfitting to any class of running will ever be seen.

To go full tilt against this mutilation of correct running principles, there must be shown a comparison between the striding caused by the right and the wrong ways of carrying the arms. Just place your arms at your sides, put your two feet together, toeing a mark on the ground, and stride out as far as you can, first with the left then with the right leg (keeping the back leg firmly planted as you do so), taking stock of the exact spot where your toes come to at each stride. The hands will come up to somewhere by the

LONG-DISTANCE RUNNING

point of the shoulders, as the arms make their lift.

Now, having tried the *wrong* way of using the arms, make a test of the *right* way. Place your hands across the pit of the stomach, and again toe the mark with both feet. Stride out again with either leg (making sure to keep the back leg still at its mark), and see how far your feet go beyond the spot where they went to when you had your arms at your sides. With the average man it means a matter of a 4 or 5 inches' gain, with the expenditure of exactly the same effort, apart from the freer and more lissom movements. Is there any need to pursue the question further?

SCHEDULE OF AVERAGE TIMES FOR DISTANCE RUNNING FROM TWO MILES TO FIFTY MILES

	THE GOOD AVERAGE RUNNER	FIRST-CLASS MAN'S STANDARD
2 miles	10 mins. 30 secs.	9 mins. 25 secs.
3 ,,	16 ,,	14 ,, 30 ,,
4 ,,	21 ,, 45 secs.	20 ,,
5 ,,	27 ,, 15 ,,	25 ,, 10 secs.
6 ,,	33 ,, 15 ,,	30 ,, 25 ,,
7 ,,	39 ,, 30 ,,	35 ,, 45 ,,
8 ,,	45 ,, 45 ,,	41 ,, 10 ,,
9 ,,	52 ,, 45 ,,	46 ,,
10 ,,	1 hour	52 ,,
11 ,,	1 ,, 7½ mins	58¼ ,,
12 ,,	1 ,, 15¼ ,,	1 hour 4½ mins.
15 ,,	1 ,, 35 ,,	1 ,, 23 ,,
20 ,,	2 ,, 10 ,,	1 ,, 55 ,,
25 ,,	2 ,, 50 ,,	2 ,, 31 ,,
30 ,,	3 ,, 35 ,,	3 ,, 10 ,,
35 ,,	4 ,, 25 ,,	3 ,, 52 ,,
40 ,,	5 ,, 20 ,,	4 ,, 37 ,,
45 ,,	6 ,, 20 ,,	5 ,, 25 ,,
50 ,,	7 ,, 25 ,,	6 ,, 15 ,,

HOW TO BECOME A MARATHON WINNER

THERE is no royal road to success in long-distance running; but the fundamental principle to be applied to this arduous form of sport can be summed up in the one word—training. But it must be of the right kind, and the training must be founded on scientific principles. It is interesting to note that the ancients laid great stress on the training of the competitors in the Olympic games. No one was allowed to enter who could not prove that he had undergone the preparatory training for ten months; and, further, for a month before the contests they had to perform certain exercises in the gymnasium, under the eye of what in modern times may be termed the stewards of the meeting. So much for the ancients. But even in more enlightened days historical facts such as these are a sure guide for us to formulate our scheme on which to build our hopes of success.

It is, of course, impossible to turn out the finished article with unsuitable material. A bad runner cannot be built up into a good runner, train he ever so severely. He, however, can be vastly improved with proper coaching. On the

TO BECOME A MARATHON WINNER 85

other hand, a good runner must be handled and trained in the way best suited to his constitution, action, and so forth to bring out all that is best in him. He must be trained on the right lines. This is essential in all athletics, and especially so in long-distance races. To neglect training is simply asking for failure. A systematic course of training is absolutely necessary for anyone who aspires to become a Marathon runner. It must also be borne in mind that this training is to bring the human frame to such perfection that it can withstand the arduous task before it; the training must be of the right kind, and it is only by long experience that the correct system of training has become known.

Undergoing a Preparation

Marathon-racing is a far more strenuous ordeal than ordinary cinder-path racing. In the first place, it is all road-work, and is therefore far more trying; the wear and tear to the body is far greater. There is no elasticity in the road as is to be found in the turf or a cinder-track. In other words, there is no sympathetic feeling between the runner and the road. It is all hard slogging, punch for punch, every step a jar to the body. To be able to withstand this continual shaking, a runner must be very carefully shod. The care of his feet, therefore, becomes of vital importance; in fact good feet may be considered the first factor to be considered towards success. He must possess a naturally hard and strong constitution with great powers of endurance. His stomach should be clean, and kept so, and plain, strengthening food taken at regular intervals. In fact, he must live by routine day by day. A diet-sheet should be arranged in exactly the same manner as if he was in the doctor's hands. The runner's aim must be to make himself as sound as possible in wind and limb, and gradually by constant practice to bring his muscles and sinews to the highest pitch of endurance. To accomplish this, at least three months' systematic training is absolutely essential before he can hope to be in a fit condition to do himself justice. It is not the distance but the pace that kills, that must be borne in mind. Twenty-six to twenty-seven miles, after all, is not an extraordinary distance to cover, when it is remembered what the six-days' go-as-you-please pedestrians need to do. But in Marathons the conditions are different, and the pace is always hot—so hot, indeed, that if there be a weak spot in the runner's condition it is sure to be discovered. In short, he will crack before the end of the race is in view.

The combination of pace and distance will be too much for him.

Medicine

At the outset a course of physic is necessary. The stomach must be thoroughly cleansed with old-fashioned herbal medicines. Epsom salts also may be used with advantage. It is always necessary to get at the liver—the sieve to the body—as the principal organ to be cleared. The first week of training should be devoted to this cleansing of the internal organs of the body. Medicine should be taken every day, morning and evening, on an empty stomach. After the first seven days of this somewhat drastic treatment, a weekly dose will suffice. Sunday, being the quietest day, is the best one to choose, unless there are any symptoms of biliousness or costiveness.

It is during this first week of preparation that the runner's feet should be attended to. The nails should be carefully examined, especially the big toe nails. They should not be cut at the sides, but hollowed out slightly at the top. Nail-cutting should be performed after bathing the feet. If the sides of the nails become tender, a small pad of cotton wool soaked in vaseline may be applied with advantage round the toe, if possible inserting some under the nail.

Foot Pickle

This is also the time to commence to get the feet into condition for the future hard work. Artificial means may usefully be employed here, as the runner has great friction to contend with between the sock and shoe. Even people blessed with hard feet will make sure, doubly sure, by using a pickle which will make the skin tough. The best of all is made from the gall of a sheep and spirits of camphor mixed in equal parts. The feet should be bathed in this solution two or three times a day, until the experienced eye of the trainer is satisfied that the feet have gone through a sufficiently hardening process. After a course of this pickling it is almost impossible for the runner to suffer from blisters. Should he, however, unfortunately contract one, it must be dealt with at once with a sharp knife and Friar's balsam applied to the part on a lint bandage. It is during the early stages of the training that foot troubles are most likely to occur, and the feet should be carefully examined each day after work has been performed. If the feet stand the necessary strain for a week, there will be no fear of a breakdown, providing ordinary care is bestowed on them. Sound, hard feet are everything to a long-distance runner.

Three Pairs of Shoes

The road to success is to be obtained by paying attention to the smallest matters of detail. It is, therefore, necessary to enumerate the most minute particulars. The runner's shoes, the number of pairs he should have, the socks and material they are made of, are all subjects of careful consideration not to be overlooked. Too much stress cannot be laid upon the vital importance of having a long-distance runner properly shod. Spare no reasonable expense in this necessary part of his equipment. The object to be arrived at is to have a close-fitting, and yet an easy kind of shoe. It must be tough, able to withstand the rough wear and tear of road-work, and yet the uppers must be soft and pliable. They should be made of non-stretching leather. A Marathon runner should certainly have at his disposal three pairs of these shoes at the commencement of his training operations.

If people are incredulous on the importance of having three pairs of shoes, let them consider, after a tiring day, how refreshing it is to change one pair of boots for another. Better still, to put on a light pair of slippers; but if this is not possible, the great thing to ease the feet is a change of footgear. As this is so in ordinary life, how much more important it is for the man who is training himself for long-distance running. After a distance of ground has been covered, the feet swell and become overheated. It must be remembered that the feet are as sensitive to overheating as they are to the other extreme—suffering from the cold. It is this overheating that must be guarded against. A shoe that provides sufficient ventilation, and yet is of stout enough make to withstand the rough wear of long-distance running, is a difficult proposition. For a runner to do his best work he must endeavour to keep his feet at a normal temperature, and it is for this reason that at least three pairs of shoes should be provided, to enable him to do full justice to himself, both during a Marathon race and during his preliminary training.

Type of Shoe

Now, to obtain correct-fitting shoes, the runner should be measured for them and have them made by a practical man on a last—the three pairs being made by the same man on the same last. The shoes should be most carefully fitted at the heel, where there should be just sufficient grip not to allow any movement between the heel and the shoe. The slightest looseness at the heel sets up unnecessary friction, from which all sorts of evils may arise. The shoe must be well-fitting throughout, but by no means tight, and should be made wide enough on the sole to allow the runner to spread out his foot to the widest extent each time the foot comes in contact with the ground.

Two pairs of shoes should be made of medium weight and strength, and the third or reserve pair a shade lighter and slightly longer. It is generally in the middle of a race that a runner's feet begin to show signs of swelling (and this is especially so on road-work), and so a change of shoes will be found of great benefit to the runner. It is for this very reason that the reserve pair of shoes, somewhat lighter, and slightly larger, have been ordered. They put new life and vigour into a man. They may be likened to the military band striking up the regimental march at the end of a hard day's "foot slogging" Weary men pull themselves together and get into step, and swing along with a vim that is truly remarkable, making light of their bodily fatigue to the strains of music. There is a wonderful tonic about a regimental march.

This is equally true with regard to changing a pair of running shoes half-way through a run. Let no one underestimate the advantages of doing so.

"Marathon" Shoes and Socks

The correct pattern for a Marathon race shoe is a track-walker's shoe with a flat, low heel. As the training is for the most part confined to road-work, a strip of india-rubber may form the last layer on the pad with advantage. This tends to diminish the jar of the road, for it must be recognized that long-distance running on roads cannot be performed on the toes—a man is bound to come down on his heels. By this means he gets into the easy, low stride, which is one of the great secrets of long-distance running. Rubber may also be placed on the fore part of the sole, as it helps to preserve the feet from undue pressure, and tends to make the runner's tread somewhat lighter. The use of rubber on the soles may only be indulged in when the going is really good and hard. If there is the least sign of a greasy top on the road, owing to its being only partially dry, india-rubber soles must not be used, as they do not give a firm grip on a shiny surface. Of course any idea of using nails or modified spikes is utterly useless for road-racing.

Several pairs of thick woollen socks should always be handy at the runner's disposal. Stockings are not so good or serviceable as socks. The latter should be worn either turned down over

TO BECOME A MARATHON WINNER 93

the top of the shoes, or hemmed with elastic so as to cling to the ankle. Socks are necessary to the runner's equipment, as they tend to keep the feet free from grit and dirt which is likely to find its way into the shoes. If, however, the shoes are well fitted, and the socks cling close to the leg—with the assistance of the elastic—the fear of grit getting into the shoes is reduced to a minimum. Spats made of a light material may be used, but are not a necessary adjunct, providing ordinary precautions of fitting shoes and socks are taken.

CHANGING SOCKS AND SHOES

A trainer should always have a change of socks and shoes handy while a man is at his daily work. Frequent changes of footwear should be indulged in. This is also an advantage, as it practises both the runner and the trainer in changing in the shortest possible time. A few seconds should suffice, and the time lost will be amply repaid to the runner after being an hour or two at his work by the freshening process of a change. There is far more benefit derived from changing footgear than many people imagine. If only some of our English representatives had been aware of the fact at the first Marathon meeting, there would probably have been a very different tale to tell. Several competitors had their shoes worn clean through on the hard road, and arrived with their feet cut and bleeding. Others, with stouter-made shoes, suffered torments with swollen feet. A change of any description would have been to their advantage. A little fresh air and a change does a power of good.

Daily Routine

An important factor to take into consideration is the daily time-table, which must be strictly adhered to. This time-table must be formulated upon the set time of the race, and meal-times arranged accordingly. Thus, for example, on the supposition that the race will start at two o'clock, the midday meal should be taken about 11.30 A.M., certainly not later than twelve noon. The chief work should coincide with the set time of the race each day. This will accustom the man to undergo the ordeal that confronts him, and is far better than dodging about from day to day with different time-tables. It must be understood that a runner cannot perform these feats of endurance either on an empty stomach or a full one. It is necessary to hit off the happy medium. It is therefore essential to fit the meal-times in to a nicety.

The life a man leads must be closely studied.

TO BECOME A MARATHON WINNER 95

"Early to bed and early to rise" certainly applies here. It is an old adage, but a true one—two hours before midnight are worth four hours afterwards. Half-past nine in the evening is the time to retire, and lights out at ten o'clock. This rule should never be varied. Half-past six to seven o'clock in the morning is the time to "show a leg," as Tommy Atkins somewhat tersely puts it. Everything throughout the day must be regulated so as the runner and his trainer look forward to the hour of two o'clock, which is the suggested time for the race to start. These little details may appear, to those unacquainted with the trials of training, as of small moment, but in reality they are not so. There is more in them than meets the eye.

Duration of Training

It has already been mentioned that three months' training is necessary to bring a man to his best—right on the top of his form—at the post for a Marathon race. Three months may seem a long time, but in reality it is not so, taking into consideration the ordeal he has set himself to perform. The whole of the preparation must be performed by a carefully-thought-out system. One must advance by slow degrees. It is absolutely fatal to hurry a preparation. Of course some men come to hand—like horses—much more quickly than others—but even so the preparation for Marathon racing is quite unlike other and better understood forms of running. A man may be as fit as hands can make him, and yet by no means fit to undergo the wear and tear of a Marathon struggle. It is only by slow and almost gentle means of progress that a man's muscles can be accustomed to the task. If a man is unfortunate enough not to have sufficient leisure at his disposal to cast everything aside except his training, he is naturally handicapped. A working man has to confine his preparation to the morning or the evening. He can, however, do himself a power of good by a long, steady course of training. He would be well advised to stick to the midday meal-time of twelve o'clock, and to do the stiffest part of his training during the evening. Too much early work is not to be commended.

For an efficient course of training a daily routine of distances must be worked out. It is also of the utmost importance to have a time standard drawn up. This necessary detail of training must never be overlooked, either during the practice runs or during the absolute racing. If it is within the bounds of possibility, a decided advantage is to be gained by training on the road that the race will be run over. It is common

TO BECOME A MARATHON WINNER 97

knowledge how familiar ground seems to diminish the number of miles. A strange district often seems miles longer than it is in reality. Familiarity breeds contempt, and it is this knowledge of a locality that is a great assistance to long-distance running. But no matter where the work is carried out, it should always be checked by the watch. The clock is the only reliable guide as to what a runner is really doing. Slow and sure is a golden maxim at the start. A bit behind schedule time for the first few miles—especially during the early stages of the training—does not matter. It leaves a reserve to work upon at the finish. Therefore, when making out the schedule, the beginning should be made easy for the runner. It is a good plan to humour him, as it were, until he warms up to his work. Later on he is sure to fall into his natural stride. This will form a good criterion to the setting of what may be called the time limit of the miles. When fixing them during the early stages of training, it is permissible to err on the side of leniency until practical experience indicates that somewhat faster times may be adopted.

What Training Means

To derive the greatest benefit from training, a man must throw his whole heart into the work.

He must think and live for nothing else. The mind, or rather let it be called will-power, counts almost as much as physical fitness. For instance, take two runners equally matched as far as condition and ability are concerned. It is Lombard Street to the proverbial farthing on the one with the greater determination, especially over a distance like the Marathon course.

Training really means making the muscles of the body accustomed to perform extraordinary feats of hardship, and preparing the runner in every respect for the great task ahead. He trains in order to prepare himself for the day of the race, and to make himself fit in all respects. He must do everything in his power to better his condition. He must enter on his task with a great determination to do his very best and never to become disheartened with early failures. Training is useless unless the runner makes up his mind to run the race out to the bitter end, and stick closely to the time schedule arranged for each mile. More than that, the schedule will help to keep his mind fixed on the work—so it will assist him in both his head and legs. Think of the crass stupidity of most of the British competitors in the London Olympic Marathon having no set time schedule. This fact alone indicates how ill prepared they were for the contest. Unless a man knows the value of times, he knows nothing about any form of running. Only a very exceptional athlete will get successfully through or even near the front rank, without a time schedule.

Preliminary Training

The golden rule to be observed by a runner is to make up his mind to do his work systematically. Above all things, he must thoroughly understand the nature of the work he has set himself to perform. During the early stages, when undergoing a course of physic and the hardening process of preparing his feet, he should do gentle road exercise twice a day. Starting with mile runs for the first two days, he can then do a couple of miles, still keeping at a slow pace for the two following days. The distance can then be raised to 3 miles, and by the end of ten days' preliminary course a run of 5 miles may be undertaken. If the runner comes successfully through this "recruits'" course, showing a clean bill of health, and to all appearance is thriving on the work both mentally and physically, more serious work can then be contemplated. It is essentially part of the trainer's duty to make his charge interested in the daily programme. A runner with the grim determination of a Marathon performer, even if he has no trainer and has to do his work alone, should accustom himself to do his own clocking, running with a watch attached to him. This will encourage him and keep his mind occupied, checking himself mile by mile against schedule time.

There should be a perfect understanding between the runner and the trainer as to what time per mile is a strain on the runner. This knowledge must be obtained so as to know the natural pace combined with comparatively small effort. They must both make sure that the time schedule they set themselves for the full Marathon course enables them to finish.

When the strong work is commenced, good, steady runs of 3, then 5, then 7, 10, 15 up to 20 miles must be undertaken.

The times must be carefully checked by the watch and the records entered daily in a book. The 3 miles will naturally be covered proportionally faster than the 5, and so on. Of the first work of this more serious work, the longest distance attempted should be 7 miles. As a test, try how a standard of 15 minutes 30 seconds to 16 minutes for the 3 miles will suit. The first mile should not be run faster than $5\frac{1}{2}$ minutes. The second mile should be a trifle the faster of the three. But the runner must be careful not to run himself to a standstill; he must always have in mind the necessity of finishing. If he finds he is going too fast at any point, he must slacken off to what he feels he can do. The rate up to this time should be checked and analysed after the run. For the 5 miles the standard should be set at 27 to $27\frac{1}{2}$ minutes. A first mile of about 5 minutes 45 seconds will do here, and the mileage time should gradually drop a few seconds at each mile up to the fifth.

Practice Schedules

It must be noted that the time schedules now being dealt with are for practice only and not for the race itself. It will be seen that the schedule is increased from 3 to 5 miles—$15\frac{1}{2}$ to 16 minutes for the 3, and 27 to $27\frac{1}{2}$ minutes for the 5 miles. The averages per mile work out at $5\frac{1}{4}$ minutes for the shorter, and about $5\frac{1}{2}$ minutes for the longer distances. Thus at 7 miles we can set a standard of 39 minutes, with the first mile of 6 to $6\frac{1}{4}$ minutes, which, as before, is gradually reduced until the standard time is reached. The average time per mile here is something approaching $5\frac{3}{4}$ minutes. At 10 miles we will fix a standard time of 60 minutes, a rate at which only a really first-class man can hope to run in the first hour of a Marathon race and come through to the finish. At 15 miles the standard should be 1 hour 35 minutes. At 20 miles it may be set for 2 hours 10 minutes, or $6\frac{1}{2}$ minutes per mile. At 25 miles, 2 hours 45 minutes, and at the full distance, about $26\frac{1}{2}$ miles, 2 hours 56 minutes.

The above schedule is compiled irrespective of the times made in Marathon races. It works out, nevertheless, very near the actual figures made in many of these contests.

To put them in a clearer form, they are tabulated as under.

Standard of Times for Distances in Practising for the Marathon Race

Distance	Time for First Mile	Time for Full Distance
3 miles	About $5\frac{1}{2}$ mins.	$15\frac{1}{2}$ to 16 mins.
5 ,,	,, $5\frac{3}{4}$,,	27 mins.
7 ,,	6 ,,	39 mins.
10 ,,	$6\frac{1}{4}$,,	1 hour.
15 ,,	$6\frac{1}{2}$,,	1 ,, 35 mins.
20 ,,	$6\frac{1}{5}$,,	2 ,, 10 ,,
25 ,,	,, 7 ,,	2 ,, 45 ,,
$26\frac{1}{4}$,,	,, 7 ,,	2 ,, 56 ,,

What to do when Fit

When a runner is coming to the top of his form he should mainly confine his work to runs of from 10 to 20 miles. From 12 to 15 miles is probably the best distance for the hardening-up process. He should run twice every other day and once on the intermediate day. Thus 7 to 15 miles on the morning and afternoon of the Monday, and 20 miles on the afternoon of the Tuesday. Then on Wednesday, 5 to 12 miles, and a 15 miles stretch on Thursday afternoon; 7 and 12 miles on the Friday, and 15 miles on Saturday afternoon. A comparatively sharp run of about 3 miles on Sunday morning, with a rest that afternoon, will complete the week's work.

All these various distances must be checked by the time standard; otherwise there is no guide to go by as to the improvement and development of the runner's powers.

During this period of operations the trainer must be very careful not to allow the runner to overdo himself. As a man's improvement in condition comes along, he has a tendency to try to over-increase his pace. This must be guarded against, and the time schedules closely adhered to. Men, when getting near the top of their form, frequently have a desire to do more than is good for them. The object to be kept in view is to reserve the best that is in a man for the day of the race. The best must not be reached too quickly, otherwise there is the fear of a runner getting stale. This is caused by over-training; a state of things almost as fatal as not being sufficiently trained. This is where the art of the trainer comes in. An experienced trainer counts for much. After practice runs, a man should pull up comparatively fresh with plenty of reserve left in him. Hard, gruelling practice runs should certainly be avoided.

During the three months' training the full Marathon course should not be negotiated more than three times. Even in these practice runs a man should not be allowed to over-distress himself. If it is noticed that he is taking too much out of himself, the time standard should be lengthened to suit the man's ability and condition. Let the runner think he is doing well and, as the saying goes, humour him a bit. Make out he is doing better than he really is—a little encouragement is a great assistance. A white lie is permissible here and at best can do no harm. Explanations can be entered on when the man is chatting things over during the evening. Of course these trials over the full course must be undertaken in a serious spirit. They should be performed under the same conditions as if the race itself was in progress. The first of these full-distance courses may be undertaken after six weeks' training; the second a fortnight later, and the third at a similar interval of time.

This would mean, with a three months' preparation, that the last trial would come off about two

TO BECOME A MARATHON WINNER 105

weeks before the actual day of the race. It certainly should not be left to a later date than that. A Saturday should be selected for these long trials, so as to have a full day's rest on the Sunday.

The Benefit of Long Walks

On days when only one term of running is performed, great benefit will be derived from long walks on the road. A good, swinging stride at a uniform pace of about 5 miles an hour should be maintained for three hours. The runner will derive almost as much good from these long walks as from his ordinary work. A warm bath should be taken after them, as walking has a tendency to produce stiffness in the muscles of the leg.

Hot baths are preferable to using grease, which many trainers indulge so freely in nowadays. If grease is used—and for men with rigid sinews and muscles it is necessary—goose-grease produces the best effects. It takes more rubbing in than some others, but its soothing and medicinal properties are most efficacious, and it is one of the few greases that really works its way below the skin. When hot baths are taken it is as well to include a little of the pickle already mentioned, for fear of the softening action of hot water on the feet.

A Past Experience

The late George Littlewood is a fine example of an old-timer in long-distance races. Slow and sure was his motto during training, and he was an object-lesson in how quietly a pedestrian should enter on his preparation.

The famous Sheffielder walked 531 miles and go-as-you-please $623\frac{1}{2}$ miles in different six days' races. He was a great man in his day, and an insufficient preparation alone brought about his defeat by another splendid old stager in Charles Rowell in a six days' contest at the Royal Aquarium, Westminster. At the second attempt, however, Littlewood left nothing to chance. To all intents and purposes he trained for six months, and then decisively beat Rowell. Steadiness at the commencement, and dogged hard work right up to a day or two before the race, was the feature of all Littlewood's trainings. He was a remarkable man, a natural stayer, and his preparations were of a drastic character. One of his favourite jaunts was to run from Sheffield to Brigg, in Lincolnshire, one day, and return the next—the distance being about $49\frac{1}{2}$ miles each way.

THE QUESTION OF DIET

It is impossible to lay down hard-and-fast rules concerning diet. A man's own peculiarities of likes and dislikes must to a certain extent be studied. No two men thrive on exactly the same kind of fare. But it may safely be assumed that chops and steaks should form a part of the diet, unless the runner's taste dictates otherwise. A cardinal point to remember is that the simpler the food the easier it is to digest. If the runner needs building-up and wants to put on weight, then a liberal allowance of flesh-forming foods may be given. If, on the other hand, it is necessary to reduce weight, the food should be of a lighter, though equally nourishing, description. Each individual must be treated according to his requirements. The discerning eye of the trainer should easily discover if the man is thriving. His general bearing, appearance and spirits, and the way he does his work, have all to be taken into account, and should easily point the way the wind is blowing.

During the time a runner is on the road doing his daily work, it is advisable not to take any solid food. This equally applies to the race itself. There should be no necessity to take food. If he is thirsty it should be sufficient relief to simply rinse the mouth out. While the body is undergoing violent exercise, it is a great mistake to ask the stomach to digest anything. If a stimulant is really necessary, it should be kept in reserve for the last few miles. Above all things, keep off anything of an acid nature, such as champagne or whisky and soda.

The Best Type of Marathon Runner

The generally accepted idea of a runner at ordinary athletic meetings is not the ideal type for Marathon racing. Style counts for nothing over this trying course; in fact it is almost necessary to look for the other extreme. The little, light man with strong, powerful legs and plenty of heart and lung room is the most likely material to develop into a long-distance champion. The exceptions will be few and far between. Tall and heavy runners do not usually appeal for this class of work. There is too much lumber to carry. The style of running should be that which comes easiest to a man. What would be utterly condemned on the cinder-path is just the kind of thing to pay in Marathon races. A man cannot hope to keep up on his toes: he must come down to flat-footed running and throw appearances overboard. If does not matter how he does it, the great thing is to cover the ground with the minimum amount of bodily exertion, always bearing in mind the time schedule. He must keep slogging along at it, even if he comes down to a shuffle. His great object is to complete the full distance within the best possible time of his ability. Slow and steady is a golden maxim for these long-distance contests. The race is not always to the swift. Grim determination and great will-power is necessary. Long-distance racing is full of troubles and trials which can only be fully realized by those who have taken part in them. Keep the seven-minutes-a-mile pace up for the first hour, go a bit faster the second hour, when fairly warmed up to the work, leaving enough in reserve for the *last five miles, when the real racing for the lead begins.* That is the standard of endurance that a man has to bring himself to bear.

On wet, cold and windy days the strain is proportionally greater on the runner than when the roads are in good condition, and the atmosphere warm and dry. Under these adverse circumstances the time schedule for the different distances must be increased to, say, $7\frac{1}{4}$ minutes for the first mile, and correspondingly slower all the way through. It is necessary to be prepared for every kind of contingency that may crop up. It is impossible to foresee with any degree of certainty the kind of weather that will prevail on the day of the race. A man may have to face extreme heat or extreme cold, whilst during his preliminary training he may have been favoured by conditions more in keeping with his self-imposed task.

What to Wear

It therefore follows that a runner over long distances should be careful about the clothes he wears. He should wear nothing that interferes with the free evaporation of the perspiration. Even a very slight difference in the amount of clothing worn affects the temperature of the body. On a warm, fine day the ordinary athletic outfit of a singlet and shorts will suffice, leaving arms and legs bare. If the sun is hot a light head-covering should be worn to protect the nape of the neck. This is an important item to remember. On a cold day and during winter months the clothing should be proportionally warmer. The singlet should now give place to a woollen vest with a jersey of the same material over it. Long drawers under the usual shorts, so as to cover the legs, and a neckcloth is not out of keeping, so as to protect the neck and shoulders. A cap also may be worn to advantage. The heat must to a certain extent be kept in the body, but not sufficiently to interfere with free perspiration. But the body must be protected from too cold an atmosphere. A few extra ounces of clothing will not interfere with a runner's ability. In frosty weather it is also advisable to protect the runner's hands with gloves. A remedy resorted to by old-timers as a protection against cold was a mixture of whisky and spirits of camphor rubbed over the body, especially over the chest and back. This solution is far better than turpentine, which leaves a damp and chilly feeling. A mixture of whisky and camphor leaves a warm feeling and gives a glow to the body.

On the Day of the Race

It must be the endeavour of the trainer and any friends the runner may have with him not to allow thoughts of the race and over-anxiety to prevail. The day having at length dawned on which the race is to be decided, must be regarded as a red-letter day—the day which the runner has been looking forward to—not with fear and awe and anxiety, but with something approaching feelings of pleasure—a day which in after life he will be able to look back upon with real satisfaction, having enrolled his name in a niche of fame. Let him take no notice of other competitors and what they are doing, or of the fairy tales always put about concerning the powers of certain entries or the wonderful trials they have performed. Let the runner stick to his own time schedules and make up his mind to run up to them. Let the thoughts of his own performances interest him more than the reputed times of others. In fact, if he is blessed with great self-confidence in his own ability, so much the better. He will find it a great asset during the struggle. The best type of Marathon runner is the one who will stick to the schedule time he finds most suited to his own abilities and not give a thought to that of others.

It is as well for the runner to arrive at the scene of action in sufficient time to report himself present, and to have a leisurely quarter of an hour for changing. When it is time to turn out at the starting-point, he can take stock of the surroundings and have a look at the other competitors. From the start of the race to the finish his speed must to a certain extent be dictated by circumstances. But it is a fatal mistake to endeavour to force the pace in the early stages of the race in order to take the lead. It is impossible for anyone to do more than complete the course in the best time at his command. If it be his fate to be beaten by a better man, he will at least have the satisfaction of knowing that he gave of his best: and no man can be expected to do

TO BECOME A MARATHON WINNER 113

more. Good generalship counts for much, and he must in the main run his own natural race in the same way as he has been doing in the practice runs. Above all, he should not allow himself to be unduly bustled, although there may be two or three competitors all running in the same interests, and with such tactical orders. As likely as not the leaders who set a hot pace in the early stages will all crack before the winning-post is reached. The main object to keep in view is always to keep sufficient pace in reserve to see the race out. The runner may find himself hard pressed by rivals, but however tired he may be, those near him may be equally distressed. He can console himself by the thought that they have all had to cover the same amount of ground.

CHAMPION DISTANCE-RUNNERS

Occasionally an exceptionally good man will come along who will do astonishing performances. It is certainly bad luck to run up against a veritable flyer, but that is the luck of the thing. Sometimes a man will build up a great reputation, mainly because of the inferior quality of his opponents. It is not at all unlikely to find a tip-topper running at the rate of 10 miles an hour all the way for the Marathon distance. At that he would take about 2 hours

40 minutes for the 26¼ miles. The average man must, however, be content with a lower standard, and if he can do the course in 3 hours, or near it, he will have done well. Say, 9 miles in the first hour, 9½ in the second hour, leaving the last 8 miles to the last hour. The running in the middle hour should be easier and faster to long-distance runners than in the first and third hours. By that period of the race the runner should have got fairly warmed up to his work and be travelling at his best pace. It is something similar to a battalion of infantry trekking. On the first day they are not well together, they have not settled down to their natural stride and swing. During the second day they will be better together, and towards the end of the second day's march will feel as if they are doing great things; in fact, as if they need but few halts. On the third day, however, the real test takes place. There will be some of them cracking up now in spite of themselves. But the men who can successfully negotiate the three days' march without showing undue signs of distress will continue to "footslog" for as long as any general is likely to wish them to. The third day is the critical time, and it is the third hour of the Marathon struggle which is the crucial test. Long-distance runners should know this,

and remember the golden maxim of a slow start. The watch and his legs will dictate to him the pace he may attempt, and it is utter folly to put on the pressure too soon.

In Conclusion

It is unwise for young and immature men to attempt long-distance running. If they do, the result will probably be disastrous to their health for the rest of their lives. Only strong, fully developed men accustomed to hardships are likely to come unscathed through such a trying ordeal. To be well on the safe side, it is advisable to take medical opinion before starting on the preliminary course of training. At the half-way stage the same doctor should again be consulted, and if he is satisfied that no undue strain is being undergone that is detrimental to the runner, he can continue in training. Of course, the after-effects of the race are often of a lasting character. It is not advisable to throw up training all at once, as soon as the race is over. The man who values his health will train off gently. Violent changes in the method of living are not conducive to a clean bill of health; in fact, they are detrimental. During the period of training a man should pay careful attention to his weight, and should be put on the scales daily. This is the safest way of keeping a check upon the state of his health. The other guide to go by is his spirits. Rubbing-down is not necessary for light, wiry kind of men, who probably need a certain amount of building-up to bring them to their best. A wipe over with a bath towel is all that is necessary for them; rubbing is probably detrimental to this type of runner. For the much-debated bath—the tepid one is the best, with an occasional cold shower—if the runner can stand it. Hot baths should be sparingly taken; in fact, they are only needed when suffering from stiffness and for the purpose of making the muscles supple. After a long run, when a man is warm, he should be covered up at once with a blanket coat, then taken indoors and allowed to cool off gently, before his clothing is removed. He should then take a tepid bath, making free use of the sponge, or a shower bath with the chill off, or, if he prefers it, cold water. When stripping a runner his shoes should be the first thing to remove; then work upwards. The sponge bath or shower should be taken immediately.

Great care should be taken not to allow a man to get cold in his ordinary clothes after a long walk or other exercise, as this is the period at which he is most prone to take a chill, with the

TO BECOME A MARATHON WINNER 117

pores of the skin open. Be sure to keep him warm round the shoulders and body. When undressing, the vest should be the last article of clothing to be removed.

In the successful handling of a runner for long-distance races, it is important not to overlook these small details. The road to success is often marred by thinking that only big things count. For, as a matter of fact, the reverse is far nearer the mark.

TRACK TACTICS

THERE is no more important nor entertaining side of racing than this, whether as regards an individual or a team. The tactics employed may be clever or faulty, and they may be tricky too. Much advantage will be found in practising the runner or the team in the particular manner which it is thought desirable that he or they should run their races. The annual inter-'varsity sports at Queen's Club provide the nicest practical illustration of team combination that we can see employed in this country. Everything done there is above-board and enacted within the spirit of fair racing methods. The second and third strings to the pacemaking are the quarter, half-mile and three-mile races. They go out prepared to assist their first-string crack in his task of bringing victory to his Alma Mater. The pacemakers have their own race, and often series of races, among themselves, while adhering to the instructions given them by the directing minds. To get the first-string a good pace and a nice place " on the inside " at the proper moment is the first duty of the second and third strings. They sacrifice their personal prospects to the general cause; and only in the event of the first-string unexpectedly failing do they at all think of their own winning chances.

Take the half-mile race as an example. If a judicious selection of the second and third strings is made it will be equally with a view to having a reliable understudy, and a dependable pacemaker, who can travel, say, about 600 yards at a speed which will bring out the best that is in the first-string. The " half ' is a ticklish distance to run. If the first lap (meaning 440 yards) is covered at too fast a rate, the best of runners will be several seconds behind at the full distance that he can accomplish if the more suitable pace had been set. It may even be that he cannot get through the journey at all. Therefore, to have a quite poor stamp of runner in the race who is unable to go faster, if he wished to do so, than what is required of him, must be in the nature of the pacemaking ideal. Get someone who will do about 59 seconds for a quarter-mile, and he should be fast enough to take a champion half-miler along as far as he can go. And if he can last up to somewhere near the 600 yards mark at the same average gait—about 1 minute 21 or 22 seconds—his assistance should be of the greatest value.

As in the half-mile, so in the mile, and farther

distances. The level-running pacemaker of very modest ability should be sought for and kept to occasional work to see that he maintains the standard expected of him. You check him with the watch and his progress correspondingly checks the rate of your best runner. A time schedule at the intermediate distances governs the whole plan of campaign, plus the strict instruction to let only the man he is pacing through to the inside position when the moment is at hand for the real racing between the rival cracks to begin.

So much for pacemaking at the only distances where it can be employed in accordance with preconceived ideas. The quarter-mile being run at so fast a clip is dependent upon the incidents of the race. This is of a middle-distance type, which, if not obscuring judgment of pace and coolheaded appreciation of position, is mostly concerned with getting the distance at almost full pressure all the way. The chief points to aim at are, either (1) to be first at the bend and hold the inside position all the way, (2) or husband your speed until the finishing straight is reached by lying away, but not beyond striking distance of the leaders. It is either head the procession or be half-way there. But there is nothing more certain than that, whether in a field of runners or in a single-handed match at the " quarter," it is best to get the lead before rounding the first bend and, sticking tight as wax to the inside berth, make the nearest road for home. If you are up against a speedier opponent, chase him to the bend and fall in behind him. Never on any account try to pass anyone who has the inside position going round a corner or bend of the track. There will be plenty of time for you to make the attempt when you are in the straight. The reason is simple enough, of course. On a bend the outside man will travel several yards further than the inside one. Make a practical test with someone slower than yourself and see how difficult it is to get by him when you are both running and he is only slightly ahead.

The experienced runner will nurse or let himself out according to the nature of the opposition. In either case, he should do better in front than behind, or mixed up with the field in a quarter-mile race. He is making the short cut to the winning-post and he is the M.C. in the matter of setting the pace. At the longer distances, when running a waiting race and relying upon a burst of speed in the last lap, it is easier to trail the footsteps of your most dangerous rival, and never show yourself until the very instant you want to slip by him. The trouble with most runners who intend to wait (in front or behind) is that they have not the will-power to wait long enough. It was in this way that Jean Bouin the wonderful young Frenchman, lost that most stirring 5000 metres race in the Stockholm Olympic Games to the equally marvellous Finn, Hannes Kohlemainen. Only the impatience of the Frenchman caused his defeat. Stronger and clearly faster than the Finn, he took the lead and kept it, while his gallant rival was storming and raging away behind him in a vain endeavour to get by. Bouin had the inside berth by virtue of his superior sprinting ability, and he kept there until a little more than half-way round the last lap. At the beginning of the last bend he could wait no longer and bolted for home. He soon set up a five or six yards lead. He was well in front midway through the finishing straight. But he had made his effort too soon. Had he saved it until fifty yards from the tape and kept the indomitable Finn (as this tenacious runner was willing to do) racing outside him on that last bend, another result than the surpassing victory of Kohlemainen would have been attained. Bouin could give the winner 3 or 4 yards start in 100 yards, but he could not last the final 200 yards through at top pressure. And near home he faltered and swerved to let the Finnish prodigy win one of the greatest races written in the annals of athletic history.

TRACK TACTICS

The only track tactics in sprinting are to take a few short runs out along your stringed track for the double purpose of seeing that the path is in proper order and stimulating the circulation; to wear long drawers and gloves (in very cold weather) and not remove them until it is time to get on the mark. A mixture of spirits of camphor and raw alcohol rubbed over the body and legs is a fine preventive against cold. Once at the mark concentrate all your attention on some point right behind the winning-posts and in line with your track. Keep your eyes fixed on this from the time your ears catch the crack of the pistol until you are well through the worsted. In this way, you will run straight and lose as little ground as possible in getting home. A great sprinting fault is looking about one, or easing off and getting the body too upright, during a race. They are next door to turning the head round to watch what the others are doing—often a fatal mistake. Always keep your correct position and run straight out.

One other sprinting artifice which must not be overlooked is making the best of your way against a wind blowing in the runner's face, or at the side of him. Get the head down low and more forward than the usual pitch when the wind is dead against you, and lean over towards it when it comes sideways at you. In the first instance, by keeping the head and shoulders down you avoid some of the pressure owing to the fact that the wind usually loses force as it nears the ground. Then, by leaning against a side-wind—and the more powerful this is, the more weight you put into the effort—one averts the likelihood (always present with the light, leggy stamp of runner) of being put right off the running balance and thrown out of stride.

In distance-running, unless you are of the big and strong class of runners, or vastly superior to your opponents, get right in behind the leader and time your finishing burst so that you steal a march on them all, and watch that none do so to you.

Racing tactics tell, of course, more with teams than with individual runners. Let the apologists say what they like, and talk of spoiling the international brotherhood arrived at by the revival of the Olympic games—a splendid ideal which they may yet fulfil—the writer feels the necessity of presenting by diagrams the methods adopted by various teams in recent quarter-mile, half-mile and one-mile races. The first of these occurred at the memorable 1908 games in London, and the second and third named at Stockholm in 1912. In neither instance is there a desire to unduly colour the picture nor aught of malice intended in the reproduction of the then much-discussed " team-work " of the Americans, who were doubtless right according to their own lights and practices.

The famous " Halswelle incident " occurred in connexion with the quarter-mile example. There were four runners in the final heat, three Americans and the Britisher, Halswelle, who was expected to win pretty easily. He would have done so, but for the extremely unwise directions of the multitudinous advisers thronging the dressing-room. These advised him to go all out for record from the very start. The wiser counsel of experienced men suggested that the Britisher, not having the sprinting pace of his rivals, should wait until the abnormally long finishing straight (about 180 yards in length) before letting himself go all out. Unfortunately, as is usually the case, the voices of the uninitiated majority (which included those of not a few well meaning people who still loom large in the world of English athletics) determined the tactics. As a consequence, Halswelle was easily led and carried out at the bend by first one and then the other of two faster rivals. Trying to round them he travelled right to the outside of the track, losing many yards in doing so, and (as the race was run) he was not first at the tape. The writer reserves his opinion as to the rights or wrongs of breaking the tape and asking the race to be run a second time with *stringed tracks for each runner*. He would merely ask a little consideration of the diagram illustrating the affair.

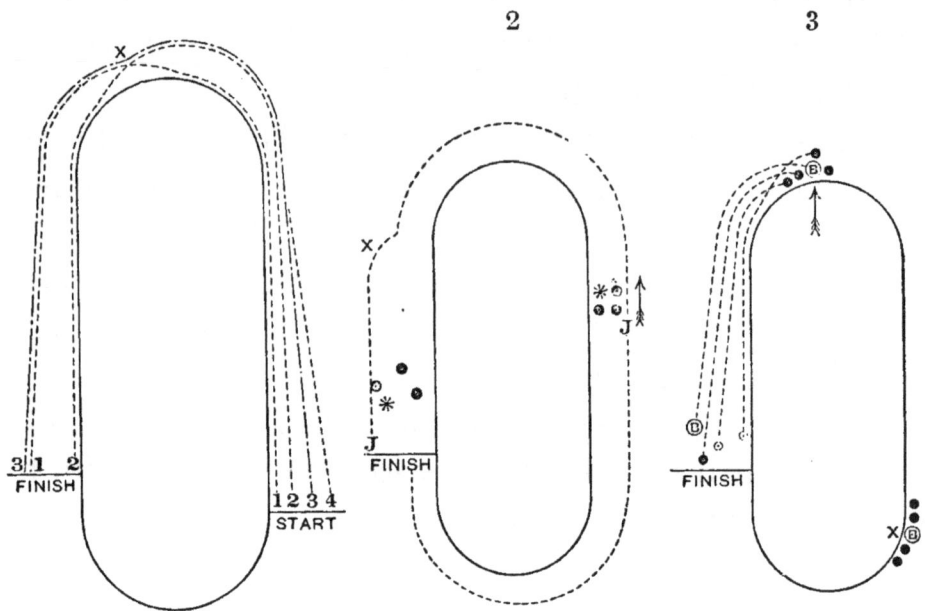

DIAGRAM 1.—The memorable "Halswelle" incident reproduced. Nos. 1, 2 and 4 indicate the American competitors, and No. 3 shows Halswelle's position. No. 1 was first away, followed by No. 2, who took his close attendant (No. 3) very wide at the first bend. No. 3 eventually wrestled by, only to be "blanketed" by No. 1 at the spot marked with an × and carried right out of his ground, while No. 2 (exchanging positions with No. 1) dexterously slipped through to the inside station and made the nearest way home.

DIAGRAM 2.—The dotted line shows the course that A. N. S. Jackson (denoted by a J) was forced to take around the whole of the last lap after having had to run outside his field in the three preceding laps. The American quad (with the crack, Kiviat, starred and well shielded) formation is indicated beside the → and the × tells where Jackson made his finishing spurt and rounded the opposition.

DIAGRAM 3.— × How Braun (whose position is marked by a ringed B) was surrounded or "pocketed" for three-fourths of the distance → where he broke clear at the finish bend. His course will show how he was taken the farthest way round, and that his outside attendant was allowed to get the coveted inside berth in the run home to the winning-posts.

TRACK TACTICS

Sitting out the splendidly contested races at Stockholm, fully conscious of the outstanding merits of the American team, both in individual and team ability, the old hand could not help but conjure up reminiscences of the Shepherd's Bush stadium in observing its well-disciplined actions. Personal ambitions vanished. The team first, and everything else dropped out of mind. That is how the Americans entered upon the Stockholm Olympiad. I do not in any way blame the youngsters themselves who took part in the races, nor wish to make too much capital of two incidents which were unfavourable, first, to an English and then to a German runner. In both instances, the tactics were clearly mapped out by older heads and long before the time for the races came along. They were mostly brought about by the fact of the strong American representation in the final heats.

Take the Stockholm mile. Here A. N. S. Jackson must have covered a full 50 yards more ground than any of his nearest attendants in that stirring finish which will never fade out of the memory of one man who witnessed it. The combination of the Americans must not be described as unfair, greatly as it assisted the winning chances of their own best man (Kiviat) and rendered Jackson's already difficult task doubly so. Plainly trying to get the lead at the start, but being outpaced in the short sprint to the first bend, he had to try to fall in where he could in the moving file of runners. But he could not get a place, and he remained outside them, doing the best he could for himself until the chivalrous Cantab, P. J. Baker (setting an example of unrehearsed pacemaking such as may never be equalled among classical foot-runners), piloted him wide of the living string, winding its way around the congested inside edge of the track. Jackson was never at any time in an inside berth, and he and Baker were travelling yards farther than the remainder of the field at each lap.

Just before the signal bell denoting the last lap was sounded, an American rush to the front was seen. Four wearers of the starred and striped badges spurted and took up a well-conceived shielding formation of a quartet racing in two pairs packed closely together, with the fastest man, Kiviat, in the inside berth. Jackson took close order with them, lying just on the right of the rear pair. He was pretty nearly out in the middle of the track and going further out of his ground than ever. Around the leading five men went until the finishing straight was reached. With consummate judgment for one so comparatively unversed in racing experience, Jackson had reserved his effort. Now, he let himself go, and those giant strides brought him up level with, and gradually by, those four struggling and game wearers of the American colours. One at a time, then altogether, they tried to hold him, but he held on to win a wonderful race and set the eyes of those who know a great runner when they see him blazing with an enthusiastic fire that did not quickly smoulder. None but a surpassing champion could have won in the face of the astute (but fair) tactics pursued against him.

Another very great runner, the German Hans Braun, lost a race which, on his previous performances he might have won. Force of circumstances, however, proved all too strong for him. On a circumscribed track, and among a large field of runners, each and all striving for his own ends in one of the fastest races at the distance ever seen, the German was a sufferer in the 800 metres race. He was very uncomfortably boxed up when he could have been making good use of himself, once all but cut off his feet, and finally made to go very wide and try to get by on a bend. To a long-striding runner there is nothing so disturbing as being tied-up, and given little foot or elbow room. Only those who have been similarly situated can appreciate the drawbacks under which Braun laboured with a strenuous and very determined posse of American rivals in front, beside and behind him. He was in a " pocket " and unable to extricate himself.

Again a very definite line of conduct was pursued by the American competitors, who formed the great majority in this final heat. A top-speed dash to the front and a single-file procession as soon as all had fairly settled down saw Braun pushing ahead and momentarily showing at the head of affairs, with much confusion and jostling at the corners as the men tried to take their positions. So he fell into third place, where he was joined on his right hand by a very watchful and patient rival—undoubtedly the best of the American contingent, whose orders evidently took the form of urging him to be with the German wherever the latter was placed. Packed in behind two very fast rival pacemakers, having other rivals at his heels and beside him, Braun was indeed in a tight fix. Worried and uncertain how long he would remain boxed in, he committed an indiscretion about 150 yards (perhaps a trifle more than this) from the finish which may have cost him the race, although he had had a lot taken out of him by under-striding (as tiring as over-striding) while hampered amidst the living train. If Braun jeopardized his own chances, he completely ruined that of his side attendant. In a frantic

TRACK TACTICS 131

dash to get clear, the German quite unintentionally (and naturally) gave the latter the full force of an elbow right in the chest.

As the outcome, Braun unwisely (no doubt in a spirit of irritation) tried to race by the two leaders, who sheered out away from the inside berth, automatically taking him with them. The recipient of the elbow, knocked out of his stride, momentarily fell some ten yards behind.

There is little room for doubt as to his high quality, as, but for the check he sustained, this good runner proved that he would have surely been a match even for Braun by actually getting within a yard of the winner. His defeat may be attributed to the acute development of tactics ordered before the runners came out upon the track equally with their adverse effect upon the chance of Braun. If serving no other good purpose, they may be here set forth to call attention to the material fact that when there are several runners in the same interest, there must be a definite plan of campaign. This plan can only be founded on the lines of tackling the best of the opposition in a manner least suited to his way of running races while maintaining a due regard for one's own requirements. Braun took his revenge the next day (when, as a precaution, stringed tracks for each of the runners were laid out), by defeating, not to say running away from, his conqueror of the previous day and so supporting a vivid impression of what should have been.

As clear a presentation of the three detailed races, furnishing examples of extreme " track tactics," as the author can give are set forth on the diagrams accompanying this section of the book.

Of course, as has been explained, single-handed matches and team races bear no resemblance to one another. But both have this in common, that the quicker a runner is on his feet and able to deliver a bit of fast running at needed moments (as much in long-distance as in middle-distance, or sprints of all kinds) the more is he liable to make himself " master of the track." Take two level runners at a quarter-of-a-mile who, running singly and separately, will show the same time on the watch. Let them run a race at the distance. If he has any head or racing craft at all, the runner who is faster on his feet can, by getting to the front and setting his own pace round the bends, make certain of getting a yard or two start to come up the finishing straight with. And should his opponent try to force him before this is reached (especially at the corners), then the leader's advantage must be considerably increased. The runner, at all distances, who has the requisite

TRACK TACTICS

stamina to get the course (whether this be 1 mile or 50 miles) and a turn of speed (which can be cultivated) to take him ahead must always be the better man. And he is wasting golden opportunities if he does not readily go to the front and make himself a leader, in every sense of the word, by setting a pace that suits him best. None can hope for more than this.

Patience, a good head and a lively pair of feet (used at their most rapid paces) are race-winning qualities which will always stand good. Many an almost dead-tired runner has just squeezed home by leaving enough in himself for a timely spurt in the last few yards, and snatched a victory right off a stronger but less speedy man's chest. But the really great runners seem to have every racing faculty, from physical aptitude to a positively "horse-sense" appreciation of tactical moves. We others can only sit at the feet of these gifted exceptions and pick up the crumbs of exemplary matter which they often unconsciously drop.

Relay racing deserves its mention, because this is a form of competitive running very much on the increase. There is method in handling the flag and receiving it. The flag should always be carried in the left hand and taken with the right hand. The upright starting stance demands that this should be so for all but left-handed runners, who are out of place in any but a very well-coached relay team. As an example, there is a photograph (given on page 34) showing a relay race in progress and one of the runners awaiting the flag is actually turned in a back-handed way to take it in his left hand. Whether the carrier is bringing it *in his right hand, and therefore on the wrong side of the next runner*, one cannot say. If so, there is a double fault. The runner on the inside edge of the track is, however, doing his work correctly, so is the man who is just about to hand him the flag. There will be, at least, 2 or 3 yards (a long distance to lose or win by) difference between the positions of the two men in starting away from their marks.

Of course the proper tactics to pursue in all racing classes is for the awaiting runner not to stand fast-footed but to stay some 20 yards behind the mark he has to start from and, getting into his running, take the flag a few yards short of there, while nicely on the move. This means the difference of a flying as against a standing start. It is the American fashion, which has brisked up the relay time records at all distances.

TRACK TACTICS IN RELAY RUNNING

CORRECT AND INCORRECT POSITIONS OF THE AWAITING RUNNERS IN A RELAY TO TAKE THE STICK. THE OLD STATIONARY START, NOW SUPERSEDED BY A RUN UP TO THE STARTING POINT, SO AS TO BE ON THE MOVE WHEN THE PRECEDING RUNNER ARRIVES

TRUE TRAINING METHODS

IF one describes an experienced, intelligent trainer of athletes as part practitioner, part doctor, and part student of nature, the outlines of his functions will have been truly set forth. He is the man who can select the raw material and properly train it in the right way in any of the several and differing departments of athletics. His aptitude must be backed by the commonsense that comes with years of practice in his craft. Preferably, he should be of middle age, and he should have gone through the mill himself. This is, indeed, an essential qualification as regards sprint-running, and, perhaps, jumps and hurdling. There is no doubt about the sprinting, however. The tearaway dashes from 100 to 300 yards are the concentrated essence of running ; and those who have figured to the utmost advantage in them have been cultivated products. Top speed is the most difficult of attainment in all games of skill, from golf and billiards to cricket and boxing, where one has to keep in good shape to acquit himself really well. It is the simplest form of all, just a full-powered effort, yet most baffling to correctly deliver.

Sprint-running is *apparently* a blind, wild dash up the track; and it is so with nearly all who undertake this top-speed rush. Actually, though, the true sprinting principles make it akin to the fine arts, and alike to piano or violin playing in its technique, need of supervision and scientific training.

At the longer distances, where artificial development is more subservient to natural gifts, easier methods will suffice. The types of runners generally best suited to quarter-mile, half-mile, mile, five or ten miles, and the Marathon course runs, are familiar to the trainer's eye. He checks its judgment with a rough trial and his indispensable watch. He is on safer ground now than when handling the delicate business of educating a sprinter. In the matter of the jumps (high, broad, long, and the compromise hurdles), there is further need of specialization. With these, improvement only comes by close attention to detail. Knack is the chief factor in them all. That is equivalent to saying there is a right way leading up even to a perfection ideal, and many wrong ones. No two jumpers, hurdlers or runners will be found to run or jump exactly alike; but the higher the state of their proficiency, the more will it be found that they resemble one another. That is, of course, as far as their physical conformation and native style will allow them to do. It is up to the trainer, then, to graft his theories as to what is the right way into the man he is training, so that they shall be understood and, thus, most closely acted up to. As examples in point, take the various sections of this work to represent his teaching.

So far, merely the practical or track part of the trainer's work has been mentioned. This is of great importance, but not more so than the proper care of the athlete in the matter of preparation to best fit him for his task. Again commonsense must be the guide. As a child has first to learn to walk before it can run, so the young man entering upon a term of training must be only steadily tuned-up: gentle work at first, working up by degrees to the highest requirements, and a gradual easing-off as the fateful day of the race comes near. A three months' strict preparation is always advisable: the first month gone through very quietly; the second month reserved for some rousing, serious training; and the third month lighter, but still plenty of good, honest practice. At the very beginning the trainer's medical knowledge will enable him to give his charge some good clearing physic and later keep him in regular habits and stomach cleanliness. It will, too, enable him to agree with the old dictum, that, as "one man's meat is another man's poison," no set diet can be arranged. The tastes of the man in training must be considered as dictating all questions of food, etc., within the bounds of reason. Regular meal-times, early to bed and early to rise, cleanly, fresh-air living (not forgetting the open window at all times), a set hour for the track and other exercises (which should be taken so as to correspond as nearly as possible with the time fixed for the race), and as cheery scenes and conversation as circumstances permit of, are really the chief considerations. The trainer must eclipse his own inclinations for the welfare of the man or men he has under his care. This is the way to get them to confide in him, and open up the way for those little confidences which often mean so much to all concerned. But the trainer must be an old hand and, preferably, an oldish man to so mask his individuality. The cool, old head still has its uses in the world of sport.

Care of the Feet

At the outset, look after the feet. Trim the nails after bathing, but do not cut them at the sides. Just hollow them out at the top. As they grow again they will fill up the recesses, and avoid those painful sharp growths which often arise at the sides of the big toes. If these already exist, lift up the nail (at the part that it presses on the flesh), file or rub with emery paper to take off the sharp edge, and insert a piece of cotton wool steeped in vaseline or good oil. If the nails are continually trimmed by hollowing-out on top, they will gradually grow in this direction, and become narrower at the sides. For tender or sore feet there is nothing better than a mixture of ox or sheep gall and spirits of camphor. They should be daily rubbed with this until the skin is hard and all irritation has disappeared.

Simplicity in everything, work, food, rest, baths, and all other incidentals of training, is the keynote of the trainer's art. To get as close to the natural state, or as it is now best described as the "simple life," must be its guiding-lines. All such fads as many self-professed trainers are so lavish of recommending, notably mysterious pills, dopes and other spurious concoctions, and "springing" a man to the hour of his race, are the outcome of ignorance. Ask any ordinary medical man what he thinks of them. Apart from their uselessness for practical purposes, they are often harmful, when not positively dangerous. The athlete must either do his work out of his innate, trained abilities or be beaten by a better man. Also this: the more fitted he is for his effort by his term of training, the greater harm will come to him from the use of drugs. Nature will look after you more surely than all the compounds invented or believed in by the false theorists. If they have seen to your well-being, and told you how to carry yourself on the track (and how many can do this and afterwards explain the reason of their special recommendation?), observed the upward or downward tendency of your weight, kept you well fed, rested and worked, what more can they do for you? The fashion of the day is to massage before and after his exercises. Is this tapping, rolling and kneading of the runner's limbs and body in conformance with the calls of Nature? Does it serve to further his prowess or assist the nerves, muscles, thews and sinews to bear their strain? If anyone supports this view, may the writer be permitted to ask for proofs. May he not also urge the contention that the use of oils and grease on the body of a man who has undergone a more or less severe physical test, and the pores of whose skin are open, and often oozing perspiration, is a direct incitement to ill health?

Massage is very good for racing bicyclists, whose performances are conducted in an unnatural, forced position. Again for footballers, wrestlers, tennis players, boxers and others who have to twist and turn about in all directions, the loosening of the ligaments and strands of muscles around the bones, the attentions of the masseur are now nothing short of indispensable. These sports call for exceeding pliability throughout the limbs and joints. Where massage can play the most helpful part is in healing bruised or strained parts of the body, or in reviving badly exhausted muscles. To the runner nothing can better a wipe-down with a towel, a shower or sponge bath (with the water at a suitable temperature to the individual, and the more heated he is the greater the need of a certain degree of coldness to prevent any dangerous after-effects) and a rub down with Turkish bath gloves or the good old-fashioned horsehair rousers. If he doesn't feel good enough for anything after this simple treatment, then there is something wrong with him. The promotion of the circulation, bringing the skin to a glowing state, and giving the blood its most brisk movement through the thousand and one channels of the human body, is the best that can be done for a man in good health. Any undue hardening of the muscles, especially those at the back of the thigh, will prove the exception to a very sound rule, and, in consequence, justify the rough attention similar to that of the masseur. Some solid kneading and punching in and on the contracted parts, and a good hot hip-bath (with plenty of soda in the water), will soon restore these big muscles to a state of pliancy.

In regard to very hot (and sometimes very cold) baths: these have frequently been found to very adversely affect runners, and upset their leg muscles to a remarkable extent for two and three days afterwards. The reason given by medical men is a quite feasible one. The nerves, which are the governors of the muscles, are unduly expanded or contracted. They lose their snap and elasticity for a time, with the result that the muscles are weakened and not in proper action, until the nerves come back to their normal state. But no testimony of mine is required for the splendid natural stimulant—cold water. The idea that it tightens up the muscles is quite erroneous. Of course, if the athlete finds or believes cold water to be too harsh for his system (as it may really be for some), there is still the medium of the lukewarm state left open to him as against the extreme of hot.

Of all the things that the skilled trainer keeps a wary eye upon are: the daily weights of his man and the warding-off of any chance of his catching a cold or a chill. These should really be his great considerations. If wishful to look more deeply into the physical condition of his charge, he may use a clinical thermometer under the tongue, or the armpits, to get his temperature. Give daily attention to the weight before the athlete goes on the track, and as he comes off it. The better his performances there, combined with a feeling of perfect health, the surer the sign that he is arriving at the most suitable weight and temperature of his body for the task before him. He should be checked more closely than ever now. Perhaps the most fatal thing that can overtake a man in training is a chill or a cold. With the first symptoms of any such attack put a full stop on his exercises and set to work to cure the cold. Having done so, restart him gently, and see that he comes back to his normal weight and temperature before recommencing his high pressure or long work. Constipation and biliousness, with consequent loss of appetite and feverish state of the blood, must be summarily treated. Nothing better than the " Black Jack" compound (the recipe is given elsewhere) given overnight on an empty stomach and a hot cup of weak tea first thing in the morning will remove the source of the trouble. If an obstinate case of constipation requires speedy relief, there is nothing more sure than glycerine suppositories, which can be purchased of any chemist.

Early to bed, early to rise, attention to cleanliness, such as cleaning the teeth, a cold plunge, shower or lukewarm sponge bath, a nice, brisk walk in the open air before breakfast, and the regular offices are the opening details of each day's work. Also proper mastication of the food, which should always be of the plainest and freshest kind best suited to the athlete's taste. No warmed-up dishes, no overeating, and a regular meal-time to the tick of the clock are other points to be observed. A rest after meals, allowing the digestive organs a good hour or so to perform their functions in as undisturbed a manner as possible, is most beneficial. On no account should violent exercise be taken upon a full stomach, nor, for the matter of that, on a very empty one. There is no golden rule as to what the athlete should drink. Good ale or stout (preferably drawn from the wood) or wine, such as claret or burgundy, according to the tastes and the physical requirements (this is where the expert trainer's knowledge tells) of the individual. For the total abstainer, fresh milk, good home-made ginger beer and pure drinking water. Heavy draughts of liquids are not good for anyone. Slowness in eating and in drinking, and moderation in either, rank among the training virtues.

When the athlete is sweating, the pores of his skin are, of course, opened, and his temperature is high above the normal state. This is the time when he must carefully avoid standing about or getting in draughts. Whatever clothes he may be wearing should come off. He should straightway take a plunge or shower bath. If these are not available, a rapid cold or lukewarm water sponge-down and brisk rubbing with a towel will make a fairly effective substitute. While heated, keep on the move, until the stripping-room is reached. Here get a dressing-gown, or an overcoat, and place it over the shoulders and right round the athlete's body—before he undresses, of course. Let him lie or sit down until he feels that he is beginning to cool. This is the sign that he has finished sweating, and that the plunge, shower bath, or rub-down moment has arrived. Strip him as rapidly as possible, and give him the necessary attentions with the utmost promptitude. The slightest delay may cause him to take a chill. When cooled down a sponge-douche from head to foot (if he has not had a plunge or a shower) with tepid water, and careful wiping with a clean, dry towel, will get him prepared for the hand or glove rubbing. Remember this, however, that some men require rubbing and others do not. It reduces weight, and though beneficial to the fleshy heavyweights, or the thickly built types, is often very weakening to the slim lightweights, who really require building-up. An occasional sweat will do these last no harm, so long as they find their normal weight by the next day.

The sprinters, jumpers, hurdlers and hammer-throwers are always a source of anxiety to the trainer. Having mostly to do their work at top pressure, they are liable to breakdowns, strains and bruises, aches and pains, which the more sedate athletic departments are comparatively seldom troubled with. The complete breakdown can only be cured by rest. It is usually caused by bursting the sheath of a muscle at the back of the thigh. There is the less-frequent case of the big main tendon, which runs up the back of the leg behind the ankle. This is always a sensitive part with sprinters and all runners who get right up on their toes. The use of goose grease, mutton fat or the really good embrocations, well rubbed in, will do much to avert this source of pain and inconvenience. In some very obstinate cases of the kind a strong horse blister or a mustard plaster have been used with gratifying results. The chief safeguard is, however, gentle work, until no effort, however great, will be felt there. Hand-rubbing (not pulling the muscles about) will be found very soothing all over the legs up to the time that they are tuned-up to their work. From this stage onwards, it is unwise to interfere with the natural state, except to give them a light rub over with a towel after exercise. What has to be borne in mind is the fact that cricketers, tennis, hockey and football players get to a high pitch of physical fitness with little more

TRUE TRAINING METHODS 147

than the primitive rub-down when they are sweating and (if they can get it) a cold shower. And they need to be very sound in wind and limb to get through these exacting games.

For strains and bruises, rheumaticky twinges or nervous pains, stiffened muscles and suchlike disorders, there is no doubt that the trained masseur can render any amount of good service. Yet, if the full circulation is kept alive, by getting the skin in a glow and bringing the blood to the surface, little else is really needed. In using any healing oils, grease or fats, the receptiveness of the skin will be accelerated and increased if it is first rubbed with hot water to open the pores. The oils should also be warmed, as to put them on cold would simply shut the pores again and make the process of rubbing them in doubly difficult. A hot fomentation for bruises and strains and a painting of iodine, a liniment which eats up the congealed blood and may thereby arrest possible blood-poisoning, is also to be recommended.

If possible, never walk with a limp, but just keep to the ordinary even strides. To "favour" a strained limb means a certain increase in the length of its being out of service. On the other hand, if the breakdown is really a bad one, complete rest is the only remedy.

There will be times when complaints may be

heard of body ricks or twists. No surer sign can be had than this that the training has been forced, the carriage of the runner bad and he has over-exerted himself. You expect the hammer-throwers, with their whirling movements, or the shot-putters, putting all their energies into a cast, or the jumpers, to occasionally hurt themselves bodily. No runner carrying himself properly—that is, loosely and in the requisite compact position—should do so. Any body strains demand immediate and careful attention. Rest is again the chief factor towards recovery. But there is no doubt that here again the skilled masseur's knowledge of anatomy will assist towards a cure. Unskilled treatment may do more harm than good.

In all respects, the work of the trainer calls for a conscientious interest in the health and doings of his charges. There are men able to train themselves, to a certain extent, out of their own enthusiasm and careful mode of living. They cannot see themselves, however. Arguing from the other side, they have the advantage of knowing their own feelings. But it will be found that the athlete who can do full justice to himself in every needful particular is few and far between. In any case, he will need at the outset of his career to be taught the rudiments of what he aspires to shine in. Then

TRUE TRAINING METHODS 149

he may gradually gain the needed experience and give proof (as others have done before) that he is well able to understand his own special requirements, whatever those of others may be. The real thing, after all is said and done, is to have the youngster of the right physical stamp with the determination to succeed. Let him live the simple, cleanly life and never overdo his work after he has been put in the right way by one competent to show and explain the reason of his teachings. Thus, there is no bar to the intelligent young man fending for himself, once he has been grounded in the theory of the particular department of athletics he aspires to rise in.

There is something about training walks that must be understood to be appreciated. A sprinter only needs very little walking, and that at a nice, free pace, letting the shoulders, arms, and hips swing as freely as possible. Come down on the broad of the foot and not by the heel and toe, stiff-legged methods of the race-walking fraternity. Remember that it is as bad (and almost as tiring) to walk too slowly as to walk too fast. The middle-distance and mile runners, with whom walking forms no inconsiderable part of the training, should also aim at looseness and a nice, easy gait. You can help or hinder your running, according to the way you go about your walks. Four to five miles an hour, moving every part of the body, is the thing to aim at.

It is on the eve and the day of the race that the athlete wants quiet, attention and encouragement. The more his mind is now taken off his task the better. If he is one of the determined stamp he will long before have formed his resolutions as to how he will carry himself in the race. When he goes out to the starting-post it will all come to him. A little nervousness at this time, providing he loses it (as he will do, if he is a good, resolute runner), is only natural. But the reaction will come to him when he hears the "Set!" or "Get ready!" He has other matters to think about, then, than worrying about the result.

All runners are not of this type by any means. There are some who can never reproduce their practice form in the stress of a race, especially in a final heat. As the day is neared, they are uneasy. Restless at night and unable to take their food in a normal way, they are a source of the utmost trouble and anxiety to all concerned. They may run extraordinarily well, or (as is the more likely) simply fail completely. In any case, the trainer of such fretful runners has a thankless task.

Before he goes out on the track give the

TRUE TRAINING METHODS 151

nervous athlete a good, brisk hand-rubbing, paying especial attention to the stomach. Rub up strongly towards the heart, as a means of driving the blood there. Hit him on the nape of the neck with a sponge saturated in the coldest water procurable. If these methods do not prove sufficiently soothing, then (as a last resource) give him a wineglassful of good old port wine and brandy mixed, or old ale. For a sprinter who is known to lack confidence and regularly fail to show his proper running, a tumbler of good champagne has often worked wonders.

For the average sprinter or middle-distance man, who has more than one race to run, a rest out in the open air (not in the dressing-room) during warm weather, or at some neighbouring inn or private house where a fire is lit in the cold weather, will be found very advantageous. Half-a-cup of weak tea (or what drink he is accustomed to take at tea-time) and a little piece of dry toast will help to stay his stomach, if there is a longish interval from his midday meal.

If the trainer or runner sees that the chief part of the daily exercise is taken at as nearly as possible the same hour as the race is due to be run, and the midday meal is regularly arranged to precede this by some two and a half hours, no more helpful schedule could be introduced into the training routine.

TRACK AND ROAD WALKING

THERE can be no two opinions as to the style needed in very fast walking, either on the track or on the road, being more acquired than natural. It only resembles

The track-walker (beginning of stride).

The track-walker (end of stride).

ordinary walking methods in the movement of the feet and the set rule that a part of one foot (and sometimes a part of both feet) should always be on the ground. The whole process of race-walking can be best described by the foregoing illustrations setting forth the leading processes of the beginning and the end of a stride.

For the purpose of gaining extreme speed and length of stride, the arm-work is made very exacting and carried right up across the chest, in the manner also shown. The pitch of the body and head is almost perpendicular, and therefore entirely different to the forward slope adopted in all classes of running.

Fair walking is not at all difficult to distinguish from the unfair, greatly as the judges vary in their opinions as to what is and what is not the correct method. The carriage of head, body and legs, and the play of the feet should easily be followed by those who are able to grasp the elementary principles of what is termed fair heel-and-toe striding. Unfortunately, however, in practice another story has to be told. As often as not it is the fair walker who suffers disqualification, and quite barefaced transgressors (both on the path and on the road) are allowed to proceed, without even a caution being extended to them, and capture championships, and lower records.

Whatever may be said of it by others, the ungainly bent knees, inclined head and shoulders, with only the pad (and seldom the heel) of the foot striking the ground at each stride, is opposed to fair walking. Equally, too, is the bouncing strider, who "lifts" perceptibly and, in reality, runs on his heels and broad of the foot. There are plenty of so-called walkers answering to these descriptions who have been permitted, by the grace of English walking judges, to take very high honours at the game. Had the further simple rule been followed, that the back foot must not leave the ground until the front is also on, some others might, and more deservedly, have gained the medals, pots and "bubble reputation" bestowed in the favoured directions. Walking races have always provided a bone of contention since they first came into vogue. What is more, they will continue to do so until the officials who pose in the limelight as expert overseers either practise impartiality or become acquainted with race-walking rudiments.

The fair walker, duly locking his knees at the end of the stride, then keeping the ground leg stiff and taut as the loose leg swings out for the next stroke, punishes himself very severely by contrast with the comparatively loose-muscled movements of the bent-knees "lifter" and shuffler. Again, the fair walker only strides his natural length when at full speed, not an

TRUE HEEL AND TOE ACTION
THE PROFESSIONAL CHAMPION, GEO. CUMMINGS, TRAVELLING 100 YARDS IN $16\frac{1}{2}$ SECONDS

inch more or less. The "lifters," "trotters" and shufflers will be found, on examination of their tracks, to get over more ground in most of their strides than they can step out at full stretch with both feet on the ground. Therefore, to put it plainly, they are trotting and not walking at all, a fact that the test by camera will always make very clear to those who can appreciate the wide difference existing between the correct and incorrect methods.

Race-walking is far and away the most exacting form of track athletics. It is an all-the-way top strain on every muscle, nerve and sinew, such as no runner experiences, because of his bent knees and forward carriage. The fair walker moves along by what are nothing less than a series of jerks. As one leg (the straight, locked leg) is momentarily upright and stationary, and taking the whole weight of the body, the other is swinging free, half-way through a stride. With arm-propulsion, swaying shoulders and loose play of the hips, the details of the strides go on. At a distance, and on a bend, the progress of the fairest walker is apt to deceive, for the reason that his knee-work takes an exaggerated appearance. But get him broadside on (the fairest way to judge walking) and it will be seen that he is acting in accordance with the fixed tenets of the game.

To fit himself for his task the race-walker will find skipping, dumb-bells, leg and hip thrusts, and bending and stretching exercises of the physical drill description most beneficial to him. A clean stomach, as much fresh air as can be got, plain, regular living, early to bed and early to rise, and plenty of track practice, with due observance of the bodily weight, are the chief points to be observed in training. As in running, train for pace rather than distance. For example, the walker who can cover his mile in $7\frac{1}{2}$ minutes will not be unduly distressed at 2 miles in $15\frac{1}{2}$, even if he has never previously gone beyond the mile. Of course, it is wisdom in preparing oneself for, say, a 4 miles race to occasionally go 3, and by way of an experiment the full distance. In general practice, however, a good fast $1\frac{1}{2}$ to 2 miles, varied by fast half-miles and miles, will suffice. Speed is more exacting than distance. This fact can be ascertained by putting in at full speed one lap (say, at 1 minute 30 seconds pace)—that is, a quarter-mile—and comparing the exertion with that of a 4 miles walk undertaken at about 8 minutes per mile.

Gradually work at half, then three-quarter, speed with lively arm-swing exercise, using light dumb-bells of not more than one-pound weight (heavier bells slow the swing) for the first two

TRACK AND ROAD WALKING

or three weeks before any really fast walking is attempted. Increase the distance from an opening of two or three easy laps, in sweater and flannels, just sufficient to open the pores of the skin and induce a little perspiration. Try to copy a good, swinging style and bring the arms up with a powerful drive right across the chest. To do this to perfection the hands of the raised arm should actually touch the opposite shoulder, while the other hand is dropped and at the rear of the hips.

The head and body should be upright at the end of the stride, but slightly poised forward while it is being taken and the heel and toe action carefully observed. Looseness and freedom at every part is the ideal.

Be careful not to loiter about the track when heated or at the finish of your spin. Go into the dressing-room and have a shower (preferably) or sponge bath after resting for a couple of minutes with an overcoat or dressing-gown round you. If you only have a wipe and rub-down be careful to note that you are cooling down before you strip and use or have the towel used upon you.

Plenty of good, free striding walks in the country roads or around the park paths in one's ordinary clothes will compensate for lack of track work once the walker has reached a certain state of fitness. Before this comes, however, he will have had to do some rousing fast spins. To weigh yourself before and after these is a vital condition. The poundage lost should always be replaced the next day when the walker considers he is down to his racing weight. As in every other form of training, it is better to walk " big "—that is to say, be a pound or two above the normal standard. The athlete who is under weight should not be upon the track. He is in a weakly condition and unfit to undergo any severe exertion.

The perfection of form is to be found in an erect carriage, little or no rolling at the hips, the arm-swing such as to put the raised arm almost squarely across the chest and the other at the side in as close a counterpart of the boxing attitude as can be.

The track-walker's shoe should be made to measure and, as in distance-running, allow the whole pad of the foot to be stretched out upon the sole. The fit must be close, while permitting complete freedom of action.

[TABLE

TRACK AND ROAD WALKING

TRACK-WALKING SCHEDULE

	The Average Good Walker	The Champion
¼ mile	1 min. 45 secs.	1 min. 25 secs.
½ ,,	3 ,, 35 ,,	3 ,, 5 ,,
¾ ,,	5 ,, 30 ,,	4 ,, 45 ,,
1 ,,	7 ,, 30 ,,	6 ,, 30 ,,
1½ ,,	11 ,, 25 ,,	10 ,, 20 ,,
2 ,,	15 ,, 15 ,,	13 ,, 50 ,,
3 ,,	23 ,, 45 ,,	21 ,,
4 ,,	32 ,,	28½ ,,
5 ,,	40 ,,	36 ,,
6 ,,	48 ,, 30 secs.	43 ,, 30 secs.
7 ,,	57 ,, 15 ,,	51 ,, 15 ,,
8 ,,	66 ,,	59 ,,
9 ,,	66 ,,	67 ,,
10 ,,	84 ,,	75 ,, 30 secs.

Road-walking differs only from track-walking in respect of the necessity to train on the road and become accustomed to the jar and up-and-down-hill movements. Foot and shin soreness are the chief sources of troubles. A good road-walking shoe with a low flat heel, and so broad as to allow the foot plenty of room to come down flat each step, is indispensable. Care of the feet and other training details on the lines of the Marathon runner's preparation; plenty of gradually increasing practice over the course selected for the race; shifting the weight of the body forward when going uphill and backward in breasting a hill, and a much lower carriage of the arms for the very long distances than for short distances are the chief considerations to be studied. A long, easy, swinging stride is the one to cultivate for the longer races, such as a London to Brighton walk.

One of the dangers of road-walking is the liability to neglect the simple precautions of a change of clothes, the bath and rub-down—and to do too much work in the first stages of the training. Out-and-home walks to and from the training quarters, always made to a clock or watch and over well-known distances, will pave the way for the longer and faster walks to come. These should seldom or never be taken over the full journey. As in all other forms of racing, train for pace rather than for distance. Above all, walk fairly. Take a walker of unimpeachable style—*e.g.* T. E. Hammond—as your model.

THE HURDLES

RUNNING at and leaping over flights of hurdles standing 3 feet 6 inches off the ground has witnessed several evolutions in point of style with a corresponding faster rate of times. Until the far-striding American, Kraenzlein, took us by storm in 1900, with that straightened-out front leg of his, which caused him to land so quickly and so close to his hurdles, we had pinned our faith to the bent-knees method. This was prettier to look at ; but it meant the hurdler being longer in the air, no matter how narrowly he skimmed the top bar. It took him farther beyond his hurdles and, therefore, regularly delayed the faster movements on the ground. The English style was eclipsed from the hour that Kraenzleïn demonstrated the superiority of his leaping, which, it is only fair to mention, had had several forerunners among our 'varsity athletics. But as none of them had been fast enough on the flat, the value of their hurdling had not been driven as sharply home as would otherwise have been the case.

Hurdling needs its special shoes (see the shoe

162 COMPLETE ATHLETIC TRAINER

section) and a particular form of exercises on and off the track. The physical preparation, nor the length of time it should cover, does not differ from that of the general running branches (explained at length in the sprint-running section). Gradual work to begin with, taking

The up-to-date straight front leg style of hurdling.

a hurdle with a loose top bar 3 feet high at first, and practising at acquiring the best style (which is unquestionably that of the straight front leg) of clearing it and the run-up and get away at the one-two-three stride. The idea is to develop consistency in everything, so as to become as sure and true in all that is done as a piece of machinery. This practice

THE HURDLES

over two hurdles, which is to all intents and purposes the first two of the ten flights to be negotiated in the regulation course of 120 yards, must be carried out at a slowly increasing speed, first to gain style and then the necessary confidence. Three weeks of this practice, trotting about the track, and sharp, swinging walks, and indoor exercises, such as dumb-bells, skipping,

Old-fashioned bent-leg hurdling style.

and a special form of leg-thrust and hip-dance (shown among the training exercises), will have put the hurdler in condition for the more severe work to come.

By practising at the two experimental 3 feet hurdles, the first of which should be set up 15 yards from the starting-mark, and the second hurdle 10 yards beyond the first, one should aim at cultivating the best—that is, the front straight leg—style of leaping and the regulation one-two-three stride, and leap up to and over the second hurdle. Work the pace up slowly, until you can do both things at top speed. Then gradually lengthen out the work. When really fit and sure of oneself there is seldom any need to go over the full 10 flights. A few cracks from the pistol at racing speed over 4 or 5 flights, and an occasional 6 or 7, will suffice to bring about the razor-edge of condition.

The great art of hurdling is, of course, to be at and over the fences smoothly and smartly, landing on the other side as quickly as possible, and be off and away at the next flight in the shortest space of time. The best means will be found to combine the good beginning and finish of the sprint-runner, at either end of the race, the activity of a high-jumper, and the bounding strides of the hop, step and jump artists. To this end, the hurdler should aim at gaining speed by copying the sprinter's training, while gaining or renewing an acquaintance with the leaping and striding which are to carry him through nine-twelfths of his task.

As far as the man best suited to this especial department of athletics is concerned, a decided length of leg, looseness and power at the hips, loins, back and shoulders are essential points.

He should be above medium height and cleanly, yet strongly, built. Some great hurdlers have shown considerable versatility and gone so far as to include hammer-throwing in their list of attainment. With barely an exception, all have been more or less useful high and long jumpers, as may well be understood.

In the days prior to the Kraenzleïn innovation, hurdlers could be seen to rise and curl their legs under them and make a graceful movement over the fences. Nowadays the first-class man seems just to split himself out like a pair of scissors opening, and get astride his hurdles like a passing flash of colour, and be down and off for the next performance in the twinkling of an eye. He is all movement and dash, and there seems to be no dead point about his progress anywhere. To the expert eye there is no comparing the two styles, one with the other, for pace, an impression well confirmed by what the watch has told.

The good hurdler needs to be a nice judge of distance for his take-off, and to possess a body balance much resembling that of the sprint-runner—that is to say, his head and shoulders should be pitched forward. This position, with most of his weight thrown out in front of him, will greatly assist in getting him quickly to ground. But the forward pitch must not be exaggerated, or it may lead to a stumble on landing. The legs should be split out as though a stride is taken in mid-air, the hind leg following the descent of the front leg with a direct forward movement, as though in the middle of a hop, step and jump. Everything must be sacrificed to quickness, which good position of arms, body, head and legs allied to dash and keenness will surely create. Plenty of practice at the hurdles, in which fast walking up to each flight, instead of running and clearing them at this deliberate gait, has been advocated by one great authority, is the way to improvement. There is good, sound sense in this walking and jumping practice.

The one-two-three stride between the hurdles must be acquired by degrees, at two flights, then three, then four, and so on until the whole ten have been mastered. Landing on the whole of the foot and bounding off it, while bringing the back leg spontaneously into the effort, the hurdler will go to his fences with his one-two-three up-and-over action, and take them on the same leg, and come down in the same manner all the way through. Maintaining a regular forward pitch of head and body, both when rising in the air, dropping down and when on the ground, with every part of him moving loosely, the arms raised at the leaps and dropped when

A CLASSICAL LONG JUMP

NOTE THE HIGH FLIGHT AND THE COMPACT POSE, WITH THE KNEES UP, THE FEET COMING CLOSE TOGETHER (HE HAS "TAKEN OFF" FROM HIS RIGHT FOOT), AND THE HEAD AND BODY ALMOST PERFECTLY PLACED

they are cleared, the naturally endowed athlete should soon be making good progress.

There is no doubt but that the one-two-three stride between the fences is methodical, sound and good for the great majority. Experiments have shown, however, that it is not a matter of impossibility for a *rara avis* to break through the accepted laws of hurdling. One very big powerful man who gained himself a great name as a staying sprinter could get over five and very nearly six flights of hurdles, and *taking two strides only between them*. His heavy weight of body finally brought him on top of the sixth hurdle. Another departure from the orthodox was seen when a crack professional, just depending upon his quickness of foot and judgment of eye, ran from one hurdle to the other without regard to the number or length of his strides. It was in the old days of the bent-knees style, and he could give the amateur champion one hurdle in six, and most of it in the run-up to the first fence. He, too, cracked at the sixth hurdle, but there is no doubt that, had he known of the straight front leg, he would have gone farther and faster. Maybe some such independent notion may mark the next step in the progress of hurdling.

His dash home from the post, and his starting burst for the first flight, will be the only test of his sprinting abilities. Other than this, he will be striding one-two-three, and flying his fences in the approved fashion.

A crack hurdler will beat $15\frac{1}{2}$ seconds for the 120 yards over the customary 10 flights. The moderately good hurdler will take from 2 to 3 seconds longer.

Now and again the recognized 120 yards is extended to a quarter-mile, or intermediate distances, over a proportionately increasing number of hurdles. The training is to all intents and purposes of the same description as that pursued for the 120 yards, excepting that the length of the practice, track spins and walks are lengthened.

THE LONG JUMP

THIS demands the high speed of the good sprint-runner, and great nicety of stride-measuring to ensure a good " take off," in addition to the first qualification of leaping power. The general outline of the training is to develop pace in the run-up and get right on the " take off " board at every jump. As in every other athletic department, gentle preliminary work, ranging over three to four weeks, as trotting about the track at half-speed and fast, swinging walks in the country lanes or parks, is necessary. Very little jumping should be done, and then only at a very low pressure. The training is very similar to that of the sprint-runner in all details, plus the jumping when the slow opening month has worn away. Care of the feet and legs, with plenty of hand-rubbing, to ease the jar which the long-jumper finds the chief source of trouble, and the regular living of the athlete in training, are among the essential requisites.

The practice at the long jump should be begun by finding out the most suitable length of run up to the board. This will differ in length according to the build of the men. The tall, long-legged kind will require some few yards farther in which to get up full steam than those of middle-height or less. But a range of 35 to 45 yards should be sufficient for all. Having satisfied himself as to his own particular length of run-up, the jumper should carefully measure the number of strides which will carry him near enough to the take-off board to enable him to put in a final one-two-three effort. If this is correctly delivered, the shoe-spikes of the take-off foot should strike the board. One must practise until quite an automatic regularity is established. Once you have your length under command, there will be something radically wrong if you do not hit the board. As a matter of fact, one gets so true a stride that the " take-off " can soon be left to take care of itself as an assured thing.

Having gained that mastery over the run-up which is sure to come by intelligent practice, the jump itself can be tackled. To begin with, set a low 2 foot hurdle about 6 to 7 feet beyond the " take-off " board. Jump this in easy fashion, taking care to rise well above the hurdle. After a week's steady practice, and when the jumper feels that he is making progress, especially as regards getting nicely over the hurdle, set this back another foot. Keep rising clear of it. Another week's pegging away, taking close stock of all

THE LONG JUMP

the details, the top-speed run and the final three strides, made for all you are worth, on to the board and the high flight, should bring proficiency at this second placing of the hurdle. Being satisfied with this work another stage in the shape of lengthening the jump to the hurdle by a farther foot. Increase the distance a foot at a time, until the hurdle is 10 feet away.

Plenty of sharp bursts of 20 to 30 yards will be found invaluable for the quickening of the run-up, which, after all, has almost more to do with the length of the jump than anything else. The development of the stomach muscles can be helped by lying on the back and raising and drawing in the legs, and the Russian leg-dance made part of the daily programme. As in high-jumping, especial training of the take-off leg, seeing that it has to bear an enormous strain in the effort of jumping, must not be neglected. The jumping practice will, of course, encourage this, but a further exercise of standing right up on the toes of the take-off leg, and keeping it taut, and the other leg loose (as it will be in the act of jumping), can be recommended.

Good form is again of the first consequence. The ideal long-jumper goes flying through space in a most compact way, as regards the body and legs, with the arms stuck out like railway signals on either side. The knees are doubled up and the legs brought tightly and evenly together with the head pitched forward and right above the line of the knees. To immediately rise well while maintaining this attitude to the end will, of a certainty, make jumping of more than ordinary character by anyone capable of taking a fast run-up to the board. The whole position is absolutely true to the requirements of long-jumping. It is so good that the final kick-out of the legs, as the descent towards the pit is made in the last few feet of the jump, may almost be left out of one's calculations, for the reason that the legs are already as far extended as they well can be.

So fine a jumping position means strength at all points, keenness and close attention to practice. It can only be acquired gradually, out of the slow, early stages, when form must be as closely considered as all other particulars. Given a good, soft jumping pit and a knowledge of what is expected of him, the jumper with some natural aptitude and the willingness to persevere cannot fail to make headway.

LONG-JUMP STANDARDS

The Average Good Jumper	19 feet
The First-Class Man	23 to 24 ,,
The Top-notcher	25 ,,

THE HIGH JUMP

LEAPING powers of an exceptional kind (and this may be estimated by the average man being able to clear his own height) are not often met with. The long-legged, slim type of athlete is, usually, somewhat endowed with natural aptitude. Given this factor towards success, he may enormously improve his jumping by close attention to detail and healthy training. His is a short but very tense effort, which demands the combination of a good technical understanding, and the development of the parts which have to bear most of the strain. A high-jumper cannot be too strong on top. Strong and lissom loins, arms, back and shoulders, looseness at the hips, and long, lithe legs, are ideal physical qualifications. But they require to be properly used to work in accord, and so be employed that they each and all assist the jumper at the psychological moment he goes up to the bar.

There are numerous styles of high-jumping. The jumpers will be found to make their stealthy, bounding approaches to the posts from all conceivable angles. The popular notion of going straight and boldly at the middle of the bar is seldom realized. Most high-jumpers appear to be shy of facing that hanging cross-bar. They go over one leg at a time, or roll over with a contortionist movement that sets their bodies at a parallel line with the bar, turn round in the air and actually face the direction of the take-off as they land; come down on their shoulders or the broad of the back when alighting after some especially perilous-looking flight, and generally cut the most eccentric capers it is possible to imagine. The high-jumper *par excellence* is he who can go straight for the centre of the bar and, rising at it like a horse, a dog or deer, go sailing over in a trim, fairly compact position, shooting the legs over in advance of all other parts. But this is classical high-jumping, which, if responsible for the finest effects of style allied to effectiveness, is very seldom seen in practice. Only the very cream of the high-jumpers leap in this brilliant manner. In addition to attractiveness, it represents simplicity of method, devoid of all the artificial straining, wriggling postures by which the majority of leapers kick, twist or wrench themselves by convulsive efforts over to the other side of the posts.

There are natural styles in plenty, and you may find out your own or have it pointed out to you by clearing, say, a 3 feet 6 inch height to begin

THE ROLL-OVER STYLE OF HIGH JUMP
MORE PICTURESQUE THAN EFFECTIVE

THE HIGH JUMP 175

with. If well advised, you will never go above 4 feet until you have adopted the jumping style you feel suits you best. For preference, select the straight run-up to the centre of the bar and the unforced straight-away leap which carries you over in one compact heap. By strengthening the upper parts of the body and the taking-off leg (a prime necessity in high-jumping), and practising assiduously at this easy height, and gradually raising the bar an inch every other two or three days, you will soon find out whether this straightforward style of leaping is suited to you. If you do not make headway, revert to your own particular method, whatever it be. It is, however, difficult to believe that anyone, but an occasional exception to be found here and there, is really unable to acquire the best jumping form.

The whole process of the jump-over means collecting oneself, as in the long jump. It may require considerable strength of hip, loins and thigh, but the fact remains that it is nature's style of jumping which will always beat (in its class) the more prevalent straggling, split-out and high-kicking, body-rolling clearances.

As the height of the jump increases so should the "take-off" be made farther and farther away from the bar. The jumper will do so instinctively, but, surely, never so well as when understanding what he is doing and why he is doing it. If he were of a very painstaking and inquiring turn of mind, he might be able to gauge the " take-off " to the fraction of an inch, at all heights. It is worth his while to find out how far it corresponds with the level of the bar, and the distance made on the farther or landing side. The really good high-jumper should be dependable and as free from fault as we poor human beings can hope to be. Nothing is more certain than the most minute examination into the length of the take-off (from whatever angle, of course, that the leap is made from), and, if this can be stepped out to a nicety, an added advantage will have been gained.

Be careful to make a minute survey of the ground round about where you are taking-off, feeling for any loose or soft parts contact with which at the moment you are springing will effectually spoil your jump.

As exercises: some sprinting, plenty of good, brisk walking, not too much jumping when you are sure of yourself, the " Russian leg-dance " (explained in the exercises section), bell-fighting and hammer-swinging, will all be found to fit in with the high-jump training.

High-Jump Standards

The Average Good High-Jumper	5 feet 3 inches to 5 feet 5 inches.
The More-than-Ordinary .	Anyone able to clear his own height.
The Extraordinary . .	Anyone capable of clearing 6 feet and more.

THE TURN IN THE AIR

HOP, STEP AND JUMP

THIS is in the nature of a long jump, but with the added strain of twice supplementing the first take-off with bounds from one foot to the other, and a final gathering-together of the whole frame for a concluding jump. As it is termed, the first movement is a kind of hop (because you come down on the same leg that you take-off with), the second, a step (coming down on the other foot), and the final effort, a double-footed landing from the jump. Once again, the big, long-limbed kind have the pull over the stiffer, stockier types, no matter how agile their representative may chance to be. Length of leg, activity, no little strength at the essential points and method are the great hop-step-and-jump requisites, which may be seen in their highest state of practical perfection at the Scottish and Irish sports festivals.

Now that it has become an accepted feature of the Olympic games, this ancient form of competition has taken unto itself an added importance. The first-class standard may be said to range from 48 to 50 feet, a length not beyond the compass of many of those upstanding Scotsmen, who mostly do their work out of their great strength and natural gifts, rather than by scientific cultivation. The ideal athlete for this particular purpose would, however, seem to be of the lighter, more elastic stamp, loose-hipped, and stronger in the back and shoulders than in the leg, given the accepted abnormal long pair of legs. As an alternative, there is the high-flighter, bouncing like a ball at each upward movement, who will occasionally do unexpected things in this direction, and cover a lot more ground than his appearance would suggest.

As in long-jumping, the matter of a proper take-off, so that your foot comes right on the wooden bar set in the ground, is the primary consideration. To find the length of your strides in the run-up; to make this at the very highest rate of speed; to split yourself with a one-two-three movement of the legs with lessening distances between them to put you in a compact lifting pose for the first of the three efforts; and to rise high *but not too far*. Here the hop-step-and-jump differs from the long jump entirely, for whereas the latter means an all-out effort, the former calls for *three gradually increasing leaps*.

To go as far as you are able to do to begin with leaves you nothing to go on with. You just drop down a half-spent force. To get the best out of yourself, cultivate a moderate "hop," an increasing "step," and make your "jump" the longest of the three efforts. For example, say that you are in the moderate 40 feet class. The average of your clearances is a little over 13 feet each. But if you do no more than 13 feet at your final jump, you will not do 40 feet. The hop should be from 10 feet to 11 feet, the step 12 feet to 13 feet, and the jump 16 feet to 17 feet.

The first-class performer capable of a 50 feet hop, step and jump will, approximately, do 12 feet to 13 feet for the hop, 15 feet to 16 feet for the step, and finish up with a big jump of 21 feet to 22 feet.

Strength of feet, legs, body and arms are the physical essentials. The taking-off feet take the pressure from heel to toe, and they need to be gradually developed, for any undue haste will bring that most painful of troubles to a jumper —namely, bruised heels. A pair of tight-fitting jumping shoes (the difference between loose, baggy foot-gear and the tight, gripping kind, which are seldom or never seen nowadays), with heel-spikes, and of a slightly stouter and heavier kind than for running, are a necessity. The best exercises are : sprinting (to get on fast to the take-off), the Russian leg-dance, cultivation of the arm-carriage, and light, easy leaping from one foot to the other, and long-jumping.

As in training for the long jump proper, put up three 2 feet hurdles. The first of these should be about 4 feet to 5 feet from the take-off bar; the second about 5 feet to 6 feet from where you land with your hop and, of course, rise for the step; and the third, 6 feet to 7 feet from the rising-place of your jump. These hurdles, which may be of the flimsiest or makeshift kind, will teach you to get nicely up in the air (the secret of length). Never overjump or strain in any way; just go easily over the obstacles (making sure to clear them well) and try to cultivate an easy style. Habit becomes "second nature" after a time. Once you acquire a good style it will never leave you.

PUTTING THE SHOT

THIS is a job for the massive heavyweights. The taller they are the better they are adapted to the work. Providing they have some kind of athletic frame, are fairly loose of shoulders and not too slow on their feet, there is no telling but that any one of those 6 feet and odd inches young men we know may be shot-putting champions in embryo. Great height, strength of arm (it is remarkable how this can be developed) and ability to turn quickly within the limits of the putting circle are the physical qualifications of the putter. If he starts out with them and is properly coached to put his weight and power behind the shot, do the " shift " from the front leg to the back leg and " follow-through " to the very end of the cast, there is no valid reason why 50 feet should not be covered in the fulness of time.

To get the best out of the big shot-putter he should receive a strong but gradual preparation, including fast walking, sprinting, ball-punching and swinging the hammer. At first, while he has to thoroughly accustom himself to the routine of the "put," he should practise with nothing heavier than a twelve-pound shot. Increasing half-a-pound at a time (which can be done by hollowing out a sixteen-pound ball and replacing half-pound sections, say every other three days), considerable benefit will be derived from taking the weight, in a graduating way, up to eighteen pounds. This is done with the object of developing strength at the required points.

The correct finish of a "putt."

Once the power is acquired, the cultivation of speed must be the chief consideration. Plenty of smart spins on the track will tune up the legs to do their very important share of the work; for it must never be forgotten that a man's strength really depends upon his underpinning.

The putter should take the shot easily in the palm of his casting hand, and hold it snugly below shoulder height, so as to get the longest leverage possible. The other arm should be stuck straight out and upward, pointing the way, as it were, for the direction the shot has to take. The pose of the body is distinctly sideways, with the back leg (the one of course, below the casting hand) and all other parts loosely set. See that the knees are bent, the feet close together and the front leg taken slightly off the ground in between each of the two short, quickly taken hops on the back leg which are meant to carry the putter to the centre of the seven-foot circle. Reaching there, firmly plant the front leg and, changing the body and position of the feet, swing the body, right arm and right leg across, and deliver the shot with a slightly upward, flowing movement keeping everything going well after the shot has left the hand—and so imitating the "follow-through" of the golfer, cricketer and billiard-player, which forms the essence of their truest made strokes.

There must be no hesitation from first to last in executing these movements. Right from the moment you begin to set yourself going your chief thought must be to get up all speed possible. The pace at which you are moving will go far to determine the distance to which the shot is sent. The faster you are moving the farther will it go. Smartness in the double hop, free shoulder play and smoothness of action, "changing" the arms and feet are the points to be carefully practised. Begin then slowly, and gradually work up until you are able to not only make the casting-arm "follow-through" with ease and surety, but also to actually swing round again with a half-turn to face your starting-point at the other side of the ring. The momentum of delivery will be increased if you can get a good push off the toe of the rear leg and so put every ounce of your power into the delivery.

Take close stock of your footmarks all the time you are learning, and see that, while averting any liability to overstep the bounds of the circle, you still make as full use of it as the rules allow —that is, by getting right close up to the line. In tracing your foot-work, make sure that you go straight at your cast, so that a plumb-line laid from the first setting of the feet will follow them truly through their course.

Shot-Putting Standard

The Average Good "Putter" .	. 33 to 34 ft.
The First-Class Putter . .	. Varies from 40 to 45 ft.
The Championship Standard .	. 48 to 50 ft.

HAMMER-THROWING

ANOTHER performance altogether best fitted for the hefty men of prodigious physique. This is no lightweight or middleweight's sport at all. The bigger you get your man and the stronger he is " on top " the better, providing he is fairly built. The best hammer-throwers have been very compact, husky specimens of humanity, almost as broad as they were long, square-set, with bulging calves, thighs and buttocks, showing great depth of chest, and the neck of an ox. It is sheer " strong man " work, this hammer-throwing, which at one time did really answer to the description, when the handle was made of wood stiff enough to stand the strain of the sixteen-pound iron knob at the end of it.

The hammer-throwing of to-day is another thing entirely, and prevents any attempt at analysing or comparing the throwing of the giants of the past with those of more recent years. Now the hammer is only so in name. But for its specific task, the steel-wire handle of the day, which enables a more tense grip, and increased rate of swing to be taken, is better adapted to longer deliveries, as the book of records will tell. There is much about this hammer-throwing business that is in keeping with the theory of shot-putting. Standing loose and free, with bent knees (it takes twice as long to work up to top speed from a stiff-legged stance), the "hammer" handle trailing away wide of him and the weight in repose, the thrower has his back turned to the spot where he will finally whirl himself and his companion to before " loosing off."

Begin with a slowish, pendulum-like swing, keeping the hands breast high. Then, having the weight moving, swing it round at an increasing pace three times. At the completion of the third circle it is time for the athlete to move from his bent-kneed stance and join in the revolutions with his hammer. He and it are for all the world like companions in a waltz. They revolve in exactly the same manner (only there is a short circle with a long one), but at a dervish-like speed, working up, through a moderately taken first turn to a three-quarter speed second turn and then an " all-out " third and final turn (these three crescendo movements will mean an increasing distance being covered), at the completion of which he should arrive at the opposite side of the ring and discharge his weapon with an upward,

SWINGING THE HAMMER

outward effort. The hammer is tossed right over the shoulder away from the thrower's sight, but in making the very necessary follow-through, he swings round to face the line of the flight. " Give it plenty of air," you hear the men say who know what is needed in hammer-throwing.

Quickness in swinging the hammer, speed in taking the three body-turns, a timely synchronizing of the throw with the throwing effort and careful regard to technical detail must be assisted by training of a kind suited to such an exacting task. There is nothing better than hammer-swinging, changing over from left to right at every other stroke. Use a twelve-pound hammer to start with for exercise and also for throwing. Gradually work up to the sixteen-pound, and go a pound or two higher; it will be nothing against your chances of improvement. The great thing to think of is the carrying-out of each detail, getting the hammer going, swinging well with it and keeping in the limits of the circle while letting it go at the psychological moment when all your strength is centred on the throw.

Hammer-Throwing Standards

Average Good Throw	125 ft.
First-Class Standard	160 ft.

SHOES

The Differing Patterns for Various Distances

THE sprinter's shoes should fit him as tightly as possible. They should take as much getting on as a new, tightly fitting pair of kid gloves. There is only one way of getting them to this state of perfection—namely, by being measured and having them made by a good man. As a rule, there will be found a discrepancy in the sizes of one's feet.

Where the shoes should fit most closely is at the waist—that is, at the sides of the lace-holes, which should be pulled very tightly together. In this connexion, whipcord makes good laces, but the best of all is a string of raw hemp or flax, which, by its nature, is almost impossible to break.

The idea of the very tight-fitting shoe can best be understood when it is pointed out that a loose fit allows the foot to shift about each time it strikes the ground. This is waste effort, taking up a certain amount of time and equivalent to running on a slow, holding path.

SHOES

A quarter or half miler's shoe need not be quite so tight a fit as that of the sprinter, because his action is more of a long stride than the quick-step bound required at the short sprints. The material, too, should be rather stouter, especially at the soles. All the same, these quarter and half miling shoes should fit so as to be nicely felt all over the foot.

For the mile and longer distances the shoes must not be too short, and a fairly easy fit. The chief requirement is sufficient width in front to enable the toes and ball of the foot to be spread out perfectly flat on the sole. The distance-runner cannot get up on his toes like a sprinter (except for short bursts). He mostly runs on the ball of the foot. Lace the shoes up just tight enough to prevent the cinders from getting in over the tops. Inattention to this last detail may cause foot-soreness, and has often compelled runners to give up in the middle of a race.

LENGTH OF SPIKES

A sprinter who is running all the year round will require three different lengths of spikes to his shoes. For a very loose or wet cinder or turf track, $\frac{3}{4}$ inch spikes; for a good, sound cinder or grass track, $\frac{1}{2}$ inch spikes; for very hard turf and frosty ground, very sharp-pointed $\frac{3}{8}$ inch spikes are absolutely necessary.

Distance men will not need such long spikes as a sprinter, their style of running bringing the pressure of each stride on the pad of the foot; and there is not the need of getting the same snappy grip and release of the path as in sprinting. For very hard or frozen ground the $\frac{3}{8}$ length, and when loose or wet the $\frac{1}{2}$ inch size, should be long enough.

Placing of Spikes

Quite as important a matter as the fit of the shoe is the placing of the spikes in the soles. It is not at all easy to do correctly; for just as the action of no two runners is quite the same, and may often greatly differ, the tread will never be found alike. Some men will run well forward on the toes, others on the ball or pad of the foot, some very much on the outsides (as though they are bow-legged), or, again, on the insides of their shoes (as though they are knock-kneed).

In all cases the use of a pair of long-spiked (the $\frac{3}{4}$ inch) shoes will tell to a nicety just where the tread comes. They should be carefully examined after use. Should any of the spikes be found to lean one way or the other, they must be shifted by the maker (the sole will need unstitching) in the direction they are seen to incline. If they keep perfectly upright, as first set in the shoes, however, then you know that they are nicely suited to the tread.

In the matter of setting the spikes to give the most help to the runner, it is certain that the six-spike arrangement, three almost parallel placings on either side of the sole, cannot be improved upon. Two well forward and close together, two at the centre, and the remaining at the widest part, well apart in proportion to the increasing width of the sole, have been proved to give the best possible foothold. Some exceptional sprint-runners, able to get very high upon their toes (the surest sign of a high, strong instep), have derived benefit and extra speed by having a short sole set with four spikes. But to anyone running on the ball of the foot, or anywhere but the toes, this short sole and reduced number of spikes will not be advantageous, if not a severe handicap.

For jumping of all descriptions, and hurdling, the shoes should be a perfect fit. They differ from the ordinary running shoe by having a narrow heel-pad with one or two spikes in it. The jumper or hurdler needs to get a good hold of the track or turf to give him a good push off for his flight, and he uses the whole length of his feet in the performance. In getting to ground the hurdler lands right on the whole of the foot. As with other classes of shoes, the placing of the spikes depends entirely upon the tread of the feet.

The cross-country shoe should be made of very stout material, and be fitted with a low, light pad, to enable the runners to get down upon their heels.

The "Marathon" type of shoe is described in the special chapter on this particular form of racing.

Wash-leather toe-socks are not indispensable, although a source of comfort in damp or cold weather, for sprinters. They form a protection for sore toes and similar mischances which the feet can meet with. These are mostly faults caused by loose shoes with too much leather in the uppers. The distance-runner will suffer most inconvenience, while the sprinter will not be able to do his best running.

A pair of well-worn shoes (with the spikes in their proper places) for practice, and a new, or nearly new, pair for racing, is desirable at all distances. But remember this: all runners cannot do themselves justice in new shoes, whereas others, especially those of the quick-actioned class, benefit enormously by them. Each man must get to know what suits him best by experiment. In cases, though, a good-fitting pair of racing shoes is nothing short of a vital necessity at all distances. The same can be said of the hurdles and jumps.

A good tip for cross-country and very heavy track-running is blackleading and highly polishing the soles, to prevent mud or other matter clinging to them.

Be careful to scrape and carefully brush your shoes after use, whether in training or racing, and remove every particle of dirt. Do not put them into your bag damp if you can help doing so. If this cannot be avoided, take them out as soon as possible, and let them dry in the air and not before a fire. Those discommoding ridges often to be found on the soles of one's running pumps are caused by the heads of the spikes working into damp leather and so putting them out of level.

Too much stress cannot be laid upon the necessity of having the sprinting shoe made to fit too tight, so long as it does not hurt. The toes should be bunched tightly together; but this they cannot be if the shoe is square-toed. A rounded toe for the sprinting shoe; a moderately broad one for middle distance; a broader one for miling and longish distances on the track; and a roomy, full squared toe for the road and very long distances, will be found to answer their respective requirements. The sprinter's shoe is the most delicate of any. It should be made (although it seldom is) with the idea of preventing, as far as possible, the leather of the uppers stretching. And there are some shoes of this kind actually to be obtained, but only from makers who have yet to gain a wide reputation.

A really good shoe is made of non-stretching leather, of which there are several varieties, but none better than kangaroo skin, the best cut of box calf, or what is known in the trade as " grain." Let your shoemaker thoroughly understand that you require non-stretching leather when ordering a first-class pair of running shoes.

STARTING

ONE of the most carelessly conducted departments of English track athletics is that of pistol-firing or starting. It is not everyone who can do justice to it, and NONE failing to qualify through the proper stages can hope to become efficient to start sprint-races or the middle-distance events where a lead at the first bend is often of the first importance. The qualities needful for a good pistol-firer are keenness of eye, patience and good nerves. He cannot have too much practice nor too dependable a firearm, as, of all the nuisances imaginable, nothing exceeds a misfire, to say nothing of a series.

The most alert personality will find he is tackling something which positively cannot be properly treated without a long course of preliminary training. Many months of earnest attention, practice and trials will be required to teach him the rudiments of fair starting. He should experiment with one runner, and not until he has assured himself that he can handle him properly should he try to start two men. Then, feeling sure that they are under his control, a field of three, then four, then five, then six and seven, can successively be started. The great thing is to accustom oneself to get the whole range of the field in focus. This will only come by degrees.

An experienced starter will hold his field and not fire immediately following the word " set," as is the common habit. Nothing tempts a sprinter to try for a " flyer," as often unconsciously as intentionally, more than this summary discharge. Not only this, but it acts against the runners getting properly " set " in their holes. The correct method is to hold the field still for about a second to a second and a half (not a less nor a longer time), watching intently for any sign of unsteadiness. The old-fashioned stand-up position enabled the runners to keep " set " on their marks for a very much longer time than the present-day straining " crouch " will let them do, and it also showed the field in clearer perspective. Nowadays, the " crouch " throws such a great strain on the neck, thigh and stomach that a couple of seconds represents about the limit a runner can be kept in this position without badly tiring.

Starting scratch races and handicaps (especially at 220 and 300 yards and quarter-miles, where the range from the back-markers to the limit men is usually considerable) are things apart. For

STARTING

a scratch race, the starter will have an easy standpoint broadside on to the runners. But in sprint handicaps he must get behind the backmarker. The concealment of the puff of smoke or flash from the pistol which anticipates the report renders this necessary. It takes a good starter to successfully control these long strung-out fields. But whereas a great nicety in the way of despatching all on level terms is required in short-distance races, compensation comes in the long-distance events, with their frequently multitudinous array of runners. Here a yard or two, one way or the other, at the start has little significance.

For the benefit of all concerned, and particularly with regard to the watch-holding experts, the starter should regularly hold and fire his pistol in the same manner. The best of all places is over his head. It stands out there bold and clear, for all to see. Firing under the coat-tails is fancy work, the relic of a period when circumstances were often made as baffling as possible for would-be timers. A bad pistol-firer will show up all his faults (the most usual are flinching and pulling) when he holds his pistol up. A good man, on the other hand, will just as surely, in the same way, call attention to his merits. The professional starters of the day in Wales, the North of England and Scotland are models of their art. They do not fire above their heads, but balance the pistol across the left arm, which is extended as for rifle-shooting, but only held breast-high. The starter at the famous Powderhall Handicap, held each New Year in Edinburgh, is a veritable master of his subject.

A good starter is a boon, a bad starter an unmitigated spoiler of races. To see the runners go off " one at a time," as is so often the case in amateur sprint handicaps, makes one wonder why the handicappers are so intent on such niceties of distance as quarters of yards, and what they think (if they take the trouble to do so) of the effect of it all. Surely it is time that a starter should be asked to undergo some test before being allocated to this important post.

Beyond all other things is the flinching, bobbing of the body and jerking of the arm as they fire. All three faults may regularly be witnessed at our best-regulated London sports meetings. They are signals that the starter is about to fire, and the cause of false and flying starts. Clever sprinters have been known to so accustom themselves to a starter's characteristics as to anticipate him by the all-important fraction of a second (not too soon nor too late) which will mean a good yard-and-a-half advantage to him. Some have looked under their legs

STARTING

to note the spasmodic movement of a bad pistol-firer who could not do his work unflinchingly. Others, smarter still, have actually obtained the tip to be off by *the sound of the starter's feet grinding the cinders* as he bobbed and jerked while in the act of pulling the trigger. These are not exaggerations. Thirty years ago, when the London professional sprint handicaps flourished, there was a runner stone deaf and also dumb —old-timers will recollect "Dumby" Hignett. What he lacked in hearing and speech seemed to be compensated for in quickness of sight. When "set" on the mark he used to look back over his shoulder at the pistol-firer. There was no doubt about his steadiness, but he was always away with the fastest of them, and when the day came that a faulty firer officiated he was, so to speak, half-way down the track to the wool when the pistol went off. The way he used to watch the peculiarities of a pistol-firer prompted the writer at the time to be quite as keenly interested in firing preliminaries.

TIMING OR WATCH-HOLDING

THE correct record of a sprint race cannot be given in fifths of seconds. A much smaller division of the fleeting second must be taken to show relative speed values (as a good watch-holder will do) to so small a margin as six inches. The timekeepers at the big amateur meetings do not aim at such precision. Perhaps they do not even know that these returns of fifths of seconds for sprint-races may mean the lapse of between 3 and 4 yards. For example, the difference between 10 seconds and $10\frac{1}{5}$ seconds is, roughly (dependent on the class of the runner), a couple of yards. But where does the $10\frac{1}{5}$ cease and $10\frac{2}{5}$ begin? Is it all $10\frac{1}{5}$ until the spider-hand arrives at $10\frac{2}{5}$, so that the most minute fraction of a second, say $\frac{1}{40}$th (which the sprinting watch-holding experts estimate at $\frac{1}{4}$th of a yard) inside $10\frac{2}{5}$ still leaves the record at $10\frac{1}{5}$. In this wise, and apart from faulty manipulation, the times which stand in the books of such records to the credit of the sprinters are not comparatively reliable.

A dependable watch-holder is the product of long experience and enthusiasm in his task. If he is not an enthusiast, he will not become expert;

for watch-holding of the only kind worthy of acceptance—that is, the best obtainable—is a tedious operation to those who do not take it as a labour of love. Many of the gentlemen who officiate with the " fly-back " watches at our big athletic functions have very evidently never served their apprenticeship for the work. If they had done so, there would be less of the "fly-back," with its uncertain, vibrating mechanism, and a greater belief in the " side-bolt " type. The knowledge would have come to them out of their failures when (as they should have done before posing in the public eye as capable watch-holders) attempting to handicap sprint-runners on what their watches told them. The practical man at everything worth doing under the sun has made himself out of his failures. Yet so many timekeepers can never have bestowed more than a passing thought on their duties, otherwise they would be better equipped and more inquiring (and therefore more careful) as to their timing instruments and methods. They can quickly take stock of what they have to learn by making a few experimental handicaps (from their own timing returns) at sprinting distances. Then, seeking a competent practitioner (and there are still such in the land), note how he handles a similar proposition.

For the benefit of those who would make an attempt at handicapping " on the watch," the accompanying table of speed rates per second of the distance covered by every reasonable class of sprint-runner at 100 yards will save much laborious calculation. As is explained, the difference in the times of two runners has to be worked out into distance on the track. To get at this, you merely measure the intervening seconds or parts of a second by their equivalents in yards and inches. Thus $\frac{4}{5}$ths of a second to an 11 seconds man mean 7 yards 10 inches; to a $10\frac{2}{5}$ seconds man 7 yards 2 feet, and to a 12 seconds man, 6 yards 2 feet. There is no more fascinating hobby to the painstaking mind than this handicapping of sprint-runners by the tell-tale stop-watch, especially when several men have to be brought together. It serves to fashion the alert, efficient timekeeper.

TABLE OF DISTANCES COVERED EACH SECOND BY THE VARYING CLASSES OF SPRINTERS, FOR USE IN MAKING HANDICAPS "ON THE WATCH" AT 100 YARDS

Runner	Distance per second
12 secs. man	8 yds. 1 ft. per sec.
$11\frac{3}{4}$,, ,,	8 ,, 18 in. ,, ,,
$11\frac{1}{2}$,, ,,	8 ,, 25 ,, ,, ,,
$11\frac{1}{4}$,, ,,	8 ,, 31 ,, ,, ,,
11 ,, ,,	9 ,, $3\frac{1}{2}$,, ,, ,,
$10\frac{3}{4}$,, ,,	9 ,, $15\frac{1}{2}$,, ,, ,,
$10\frac{1}{2}$,, ,,	9 ,, 22 ,, ,, ,,
$10\frac{1}{4}$,, ,,	9 ,, $29\frac{1}{2}$,, ,, ,,
10 ,, ,,	10 ,,
$9\frac{3}{4}$,, ,,	10 ,, 9 in. ,, ,,

The handicap is made on the time of the slower runner. For example, the $10\frac{3}{4}$ man in meeting the $11\frac{1}{2}$ man would have to concede him the

TIMING OR WATCH-HOLDING   203

equivalent distance to the $\frac{3}{4}$ths of a second that is between them. The $\frac{3}{4}$ths of a second is taken from the $11\frac{1}{2}$ man's (he being the slower runner) rate of travelling. It is $\frac{3}{4}$ths of 8 yards 25 inches which gives approximately 6 yards 19 inches as the start to be taken to bring the men together on the tape.

Quickness of eye, steadiness of hand and a goodly share of patience are needed to fashion the capable watch-holder. He must know his watch well and regularly test it and see that it is always in the same running order. This point is of the utmost importance. To catch the puff of smoke or flash that comes from the barrel of the pistol (and which anticipates the sound of the report by half-a-second in so short a distance as 100 yards) just as it comes to view, is his first concern. The old hand will watch the progress of the race from almost the very first move. His eyes will instinctively sweep across from the pistol-firer down the track. And he will be able to tell more of the details than most untrammelled onlookers. But—and remember this well—he will not attempt to watch the race beyond about two-thirds of the distance. When the race has reached this critical stage, the watch-holder will switch his eyes to look along the winning-posts and the line of worsted suspended upon them. He will not see the runners again until one or other of them strikes the worsted, which event he will accompany with a simultaneous stopping of his watch. There is no greater source of mistakes than watching runners right up to the tape. A close struggle will get you so interested as to make you forget to stop your watch. In timing, as in other matters, you cannot well do two things at one and the same time; and to watch a sprint finish and be certain of snapping your watch is a dual effort which the wise (again making profitable use of his lessons) watch-holder has no use for.

The most suitable types of timing instruments are little understood. For sprint-running the " fly-back " Kew tested chronometers are seldom trustworthy because of their complex mechanism. The " spider-hand " can be seen to " jump " or " hang " at starting and wobble as it is being stopped. This fact is of no practical account in longer distance races; but at sprinting it is a failing of the worst kind. It is painful to those who have had to depend for their next meal on the precision of their timing in second round and trial heats of a sprint race to take the time-keeping effusions of those who have not undergone the same experience. To have been among the rough Yorkshire miners and seen them operating the stops of their old quarter-second watches with pieces of string, and bringing the heat winners together to a very few inches, means all the vast gap that stands between clever

TIMING OR WATCH-HOLDING   205

practice and mistaken theory. Timers who only deal in fifths of seconds have no place when a real record of the passing moments is needed. The A.A.A. would be rendering a decided service towards establishing a correct line of form were they to grant the sprint-times being returned in tenths of seconds.

For middle distance—that is, the half-mile and mile races and the longer distances—the call on the timer's services is of the lightest description. If his watch is in order he should make no mistake. A minute recording dial is, of course, a great advantage. For the cross-country Marathon or team races, where the times of all the runners have to be taken as they reach the winning-post, a split-seconds chronometer is undoubtedly quite essential.

The weather, the wind and the state of the track can tell strongly for and against the runner and the times he makes. But a following wind will only slightly assist, where a wind of equal force blowing dead against him will slow and fatigue him quite out of proportion. Any wind that is not nicely behind the runner, by reason of the disturbed state of the air, be set down as more or less detrimental to fast time. A soft cinder-track, and above all one that has had frost in it and is yielding to the warmth of the morning sunshine, may also add another half second to the runner's customary time for the 100 yards. Then, the hard, ridgy frozen path will surely slow him off in a manner which will, unless he has had similar experiences, make him think he cannot run at all. Do not, however, be deceived by the possible crumbling, dusty state of the path (which is not good) in very dry weather nor the often advantageous downfall of rain. While the wet remains on top, the going may have really improved. If the runner's spikes come out nice and clean—that is to say, there is no substance clinging to them and the track shows " pepper-box " prints—all is well. It may even be ideal underfoot going for fast times.

For the limit in speed-reducers there is, however, nothing to be compared with the cold, bleak, cheerless days of our winters, when the sun has forgotten for some days to shine, leaving the winds or mists to hold sway and the path and air is as cold as charity. The runner (of any stamp) who can do anything like good time under these conditions is a man to be respected. Yet we have seen the old-time professional and the 'varsity athletes at Queen's Club in howling March gales or sullen, brooding mists accomplish positively remarkable achievements. The high quality of many of the Oxford and Cambridge athletic lights (some of whom, in the days gone by, have yet contrived to add a brilliant

TIMING OR WATCH-HOLDING

page or two to athletic history!) tells us where to expect our champions from.

SOME WATCH-HOLDING "IMPRESSIONS"

To illustrate the methods of timing as plainly as possible, let us "hold the watch" on an imaginary sprint. We are depending upon my old favourite the humble side-stop. The circumlocutory "spider-hand" is "dead on the 60." The runners are on their marks, their arms reaching down till their finger-tips touch the cinders, their bodies bent right over. Behind them stands the erect figure of the pistol-firer, on whom we throw the full intensity of our gaze. We search for the firearm. Generally it is easy to discern. Pistol-firers, like other people, do things in different ways. Some almost baffle the most watchful of timekeepers by "loosing off the gun" from varying positions. We are lucky now to have an old practitioner in co-operation and his holding of the pistol over his head simplifies our work. "Get ready!" comes faintly up the strings to us. We see the stooping forms of the competitors hump themselves up into more rigid poses than before. A pause; then a puff of smoke. Our alert eyes catch it. The waiting thumb and forefinger shoot the starting lever of the watch sharply its full length and the floodgates of the fifth of seconds are opened. Then to your ears should come the sharp report of the pistol.

We watch the runners as they dash towards us, and while doing so turn over the watch so that when the proper moment arrives the striking action of the stop will be identical with the "start"—a point most strongly to be urged. One, at least, of them swerves about as he struggles to get into his stride. The thick-set little man, with his strength so near to the ground, running next the turf is, plainly, the fastest beginner. His feet strike the cinders much faster than the beating of your watch. He brings the others along at the utmost limit of their speed. Half-way through he looks a sure winner. But the longer striding of his rivals wears him down. Thirty yards from the tape one shoots out clear of the others. Taking a glance over his shoulder, and palpably easing down, he comes full tilt at the worsted, in a line with which we are standing. When he is 20 yards or so short of there, our eyes, which have been closely scanning the runners, are now directed on the tape. We throw ourselves in the same rigid position as at the start, our striking finger all attention to take the "finish." As the winner's breast strikes the worsted, the lever of the watch is again shot its length—this time to pull up the "spider-hand" shortly and sharply. Then comes the examination of

TIMING OR WATCH-HOLDING

the watch; the exact location of the spider-hand; what bearing the elementary conditions have exercised upon the time. It must not be overlooked that, all the while the race is being run, we have tried to ascertain something of the direction and power of the wind behind, against or across the runners.

For the most part, though, the commencement of sprints is a chaotic hustling through space. More often than not they remain so to the end. But not infrequently there comes within the last 20 or 30 or 40 yards incidents which are a tax on the judgment of the watch-holder, if he is putting heat-runners in the scale with probable happenings in the second round or final heat. Someone will be observed to slow down well short of the tape, and yet win quite easily. Another runner will come through head back, arms sawing the air, maybe straining every nerve—maybe not—and win by six inches. Yet another will give the impression that he is cutting matters as fine as possible, yet doing so in such artistic fashion as to make the most experienced judges differ in their opinions. These and other tough propositions have to be pondered over, and solved. The man who makes the fewest mistakes over them is the one who has a deeper insight into the technique of pedestrianism than the very great majority of his fellows.

Backgrounds, against which the pistol-firer's hand is more or less clearly limned, assist or deter, according to their shades, the watch-holder's view. The most difficult of any I once found to be the raised khaki-hued cement-banking of a cycle-track which the sun, high in the heavens, shone most ardently upon. If ever there was a glaring bit of work for the eyes that was. But I "got him" every time simply by sticking persistently to my task.

One of the most demoralizing effects which can be inflicted on the amateur watch-holder is the cap on the nipple of the pistol snapping without exploding the powder. He sees the runners on the move although no smoke or flash are visible, and, half with eager intent and half involuntarily, he slides the lever of his watch to send the expectant spider-hand on a fruitless mission. The veteran will not succumb to these mishaps. He is armed *cap-à-pie* to them. Unremitting practice and memories of early fiascos keep him clear of such pit-falls.

Electrical timers set in communication with the pistol and the finishing cord are not favourable to fast timers although giving a more faithful return than a manually operated instrument. These last are to be recommended on account of their maintaining long-standing custom and a true comparison of old and new records.

CARE OF THE TRACK

A CINDER-PATH needs daily attention in the way of sweeping and rolling to keep it firm and level and, therefore, as fast as weather conditions permit. The big horse-broom can be easily man-handled; so can the light roller; and, as the heavy roller is not a vital necessity, the path can easily be swept and rolled by one man. For all classes of running the firmest, springiest track is an advantage. For sprinting it is a vital necessity. A slow, yielding path will slow the fast-runner off, where a firm, elastic foothold means speed development. Winter or summer (when any training is going on, of course), brushing and rolling must be made a leading feature.

First go up and down the sprint-track in sectional lines until all and every particle of it has been swept and the top layer of ashes is removed and lying loose. Then take the roller, drag it slowly from end to end, letting the weight tell as much as possible, until the surface is flattened down and never a ridge or mark showing anywhere.

After having attended to the sprinting straight,

as the most important portion of the track, take the broom around the untouched parts, keeping right close in by the inside edge. The brushing concluded, go over the broom trail with the roller, so that both distance-men and sprinters alike have good level going to run upon. The better the runners, the greater the need of a level path. The good men keep such a level balance that a very little rut or ridge will throw them off it. A tip-top sprinter will suffer most of all. Another advantage to be derived from this regular care of the track is the opportunity it gives the trainer and the runner to note the course of his spike-marks. To those who have made a close study of this sidelight of foot-racing, nothing more illuminating concerning well-doing or a loss of form is required.

Do not push the roller or the broom. Drag them behind you. In this manner you will ease the strain of the work and find it assist in keeping a straight line in company with pulling to a fixed point at the farther end of the straight and keeping your eyes on it.

Brushing and rolling makes very good exercise, but one is advised not to attempt the performance in his ordinary walking costume. It is arduous, heating work, which asks for a change of clothes before and after entering

CARE OF THE TRACK 213

upon it. To get overheated and not have a rub-down and a gradual cool-off in the dressing-room is asking for trouble in the way of a chill. Pay attention to these bodily requirements, and many a worse method of working off superfluous flesh and putting on good, hard muscle than brushing and rolling the track can be found. But never let a runner attempt it in the latter stages of his training.

When using the broom do not always return the surface scrapings which are gathered up. Leave these once a week at the end of the track, especially during a dry, windy period, when plenty of grit will be found to have been deposited amongst cinders. To keep sweeping up and then rolling in the same stuff all the year round is wrong, and detrimental to the quality of the path.

Once a year, in the late autumn for preference, a new top layer of fine cinders should be carefully and thoroughly rolled in.

It is next door to useless to brush or sweep a very dry and dusty path. Leave it alone altogether unless it is well watered, preferably with a strong infusion of rock salt (which makes a wonderful binder) added to the water. Some of these dry, crumbling paths make the feet and shins very sore on account of there being no upper crust to ward off the resistance of the hard subsoil which every well-laid track has.

The difference between a firm, elastic path and a loose, heavy one is quite remarkable at all seasons of the year. And there is nothing more certain than that a runner training on the faster one will have a decided pull over another who takes his spins on the slower track.

STRIDE MEASURING AND TRACING

What they have to Tell

WHETHER a runner moves at a natural unforced gait, or cultivates one set style, his striding will be made with mechanical truth. Trace his footprints upon the cinder-path and put the tape-measure over them. Then check the directness of their line. Any trouble you may take will not be wasted; for here you will get vivid reflections of ability, if you will just expend a little thought on their import. Little by little you will come to know the nature of the track, the indirect effect of winds, the loss or gain of pace and the improvement in the runner's condition or methods. All these matters are printed clear upon the track for the experienced eye to read.

At the top of his form a runner will stride as evenly as the revolution of a wheel, and (mostly) run in as straight a line. The bigger men will do their 7 and 8 and up to 9 feet lengths (measuring from the print of the opposite feet) in the quarter-mile, middle-distance and mile and upwards spins. For the genuine sprint-runner, who is all quickness and comparatively short-striding (he must cultivate extreme rapidity of foot-work to attain any degree of success!) a maximum length of 7 feet 6 inches, which none but very tall, long-limbed men can do. The average striding is between 6 and 7 feet for sprinters and 7 and 8 feet for all other classes of runners.

At the beginning of training it will be found that the striding is uneven and irregular and the footprints heavy and dull. As the runner gets freer in his joints and stronger in his muscles, the fact will be notified by the truer line he takes and the more crisp appearance (proportionate to the track conditions) of his spike and sole marks. If the track is soft or loose the sideways turn of the spikes and indent of the soles tells that he has lost time and distance on the way from this cause. On the other hand, if the spike-markings are clean-cut and straightforward, and the impression of the sole barely seen, the " going " is good and fast. Measure the prints from toe to toe in this latter case and they should be uniform to the fraction of an inch where the height of the running has taken place. Good firm " going " enables regular striding, where a soft and loose track, with its often varying nature, will disturb the evenness of his swing.

1. Good level running from the modern "crouch" start, giving an idea of how the strides lengthen out. 2. From the old-fashioned upright start. 3. How the rolling-hipped or bow-legged type of runner soon settles down to run in a dead straight line. 4. An example of bad, slovenly running. The footmarks are irregular and the strides uneven.

It is in sprinting that the fullest guidance of what the track has to reveal occurs. Yet this superintendence of a runner's work should not be neglected in other grades. To gain the clearest view of what has happened, the writer has never shrunk from brushing and rolling the sprint straight several times in one day, and not infrequently performed the same office around the quarter-mile circuit. The seeker after information and technical knowledge must spare no pains. In this way one gets a correct estimation of what a sideways turn or an altogether look-round of the head can cost a runner. On the track you see it written down by the stride suddenly shortening from 1 to as much as 3 feet at the point where the head and shoulders turned to, of course, restrict the stride. If you know a man's natural striding—that is to say, you have well examined its length and characteristics—*you can really tell more of the quality of his running in a trial or a race by a subsequent examination of his tracks than by actually watching him run.* This may seem an exaggeration, yet it is merely a simple truth.

Not only this, but the pace of someone you have never seen in action can be fairly accurately divined. A runner leaves behind him more than the flashes of wrist strokes, sinuous movements and the many artifices of the cricketers,

STRIDE MEASURING AND TRACING 219

tennis-players, footballers and others whose efforts are mostly spent on the passing air. He shows just what he has done and what has happened to him in the process of his striding. If the wind has caught him, the position of his feet, caused by the greater or lesser turn of his body from its correct balance, shows where and how. Side, shoulder, front or back winds each have their definite effects, respectively, with a sideways placing (more or less out of the regular line of progression), a slowed, shortened stride and most irregular track or a straight-ahead, palpably quickened movement. All these things can be seen in the passage of, say, a quarter-mile runner on an open track across which the wind is blowing strongly and bound to catch him, one way or another, at all points of the journey.

The fairest method of measuring and comparing the strides is to take the print of each foot separately. In this way you can more closely check the swing of the legs than by measuring the shorter lengths of the right to left foot striding. Not only this, few runners will be found to stride the same distance with either leg. They will generally be found a few inches longer on one side than the other.

As regards a straight running line: the better and looser kind, especially those with a slight inturning of the foot on the stronger half of the body (the right foot with naturally right-handed, and the left foot with left-handed, men) will quickly develop a true, plumb-line course. Others who do not use their shoulders and hips freely will show two distinct lines, one for the left and another for the right foot. Then there is the wide-legged, very strong type, between whose legs, as he strides out, you can see daylight all the way up the track. He will also show two parallel " railway lines " a few inches apart. In this connexion, it may not be amiss to mention that one may always obtain a better view of a runner's style and action from the rear than in front or sideways on.

FASHIONING THE RAW MATERIAL

IN all grades of athletics it is far easier (and generally, more satisfactory to all concerned) to deal with raw material than an athlete of some standing who has established faults. These can only be rubbed out step by step, even with both mentor and pupil working keenly and enthusiastically in union. In other circumstances, no progress can be made. On the other hand, a novice is receptive and willing to learn. He has not contracted a set of bad habits (usually the outcome of watching the incorrect styles of older hands), and he may, therefore, be fashioned to the ideas of the coach. But let it be understood that proper pedestrian deportment or field-game technique rank among the minor sciences. Too much emphasis cannot be laid on this statement.

Whether it be the schoolboy or the well-set-up young man the same careful attention to style should be given. A cat-like suppleness of limb can also be acquired in this manner, where faulty notions and conduct will bring about a tied-up, stiff condition of the muscles and joints. Work in the right direction and the good effects will soon become apparent. The percentage of athletes who conform to even reasonably good methods is ridiculously low. It is the sprinters and middle-distance runners who suffer of the track-men. The field-games have a higher proportion of efficients simply because of their comparative handful of adherents. To arm himself at all points the aspiring athlete cannot do better than practise the several exercises which will be found set forth in the next chapter. They are true to their purpose.

TRAINING EXERCISES

AS a means towards the development of strength and pliancy in the various parts of the body, the accompanying set of exercises cannot well be improved upon. They are primarily intended to fit the athlete for pedestrian tasks ; but they will be found none the less beneficial to the average non-athletic members of the community. Their chief association is with fresh air, a fact which must never be overlooked. There is no reason, however, why this essential of good health should not be procurable indoors, where these exercises can best be conducted.

ARM AND SHOULDER SWING

Take a pair of light dumb-bells (not more than 1 lb. weight each) and, standing with the feet close together, swing the shoulders and arms loosely and independently, letting the inward turned hands come closely together across the body. This is the sprinting shoulder and arm swing which sets the pace to the feet and should put every part of the body in motion. The closer the hands work, the greater the speed.

224 COMPLETE ATHLETIC TRAINER

It is grand work for the rib, stomach and upper-arm muscles. Let everything go bobbing loosely and smoothly. Getting nicely into the swing, let the arms go playing across as fast as

Arm and shoulder swing.

you can get them to do. If you are doing your work properly, the arms will first begin to tire in the triceps muscles at the back of the upper arm. Now and again, to vary the exercise, get up on tiptoe and, moving your feet, note how the swing fairly pulls you along.

THE LEG-DANCE EXERCISE

For hurdlers (in particular), jumpers (of all descriptions) and for those athletes who would

TRAINING EXERCISES

loosen their hip-joints while strengthening their thigh, back, stomach, buttock, shoulder and loin muscles, the " Russian leg-dance " stands out alone. As can be seen from the illustration, the athlete adopts a sitting-on-his-haunches posture. Having so set himself, his task is to shoot out one leg and then the other, while keeping their

Russian leg-dance.

governors (the opposite arms) rising and falling as outward thrusts and inward pulls are taken. It is strenuous work, which should be taken very leisurely and lightly at first. After a week or two faster and longer " dancing " will work wonders with the athlete's muscular development.

In this position the counterpart of hurdling and the various jumping, leg, arm and body actions can be practised with advantage.

Skipping

This is not the usual double-footed jumping skip, but as close an imitation of the runner's leg action as can be had. Jump off one foot to the other, just as though you were running, bringing the knee well up, and try to swing the rope so that it passes beneath the under leg. This is good for the arms and shoulders as well as

The skipping "run."

the legs. Keep every part loosely moving and regulate the pace to the distance you are training to run for. In bad weather, or at times when it is impossible to use the running-track, this form of skipping makes an excellent substitute for a spin.

Raising and Stretching

Another grand exercise for the stomach, loins and thighs and stretching out every joint,

TRAINING EXERCISES

ligament and muscle in the body. Lie down flat on the back with the hands thrown open behind the head. Gradually raise the body, while keeping the legs straight out (the difficulty is to repress

Raising and stretching.

the inclination of the knees to rise). The hands may, with advantage, be used to support the waist. Having come to a sitting posture, bend over and try to touch the toes (which should be turned away from the body) with the outstretched hands.

Lowering and Lifting the Body

All classes of athletes will benefit by this exercise, which (properly carried out) puts a

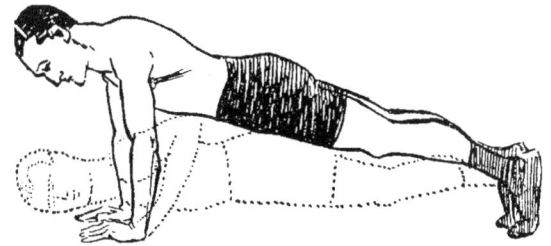
Lowering and lifting the body.

strain on every muscle and sinew throughout the body. Rest the body upon the open hands and toes (as shown) with the arms extended. Then gradually lower until the chin and chest touch the ground. As they do so, press slowly back to the first position. Do this once or twice to begin with and gradually increase the number until you master, say, its successive lowerings and liftings. To get the utmost advantage out of the effort, let the head shoot out to its full length by sending the elbows back. When flat on the ground turn the head left and right to encourage freedom of shoulder movement.

Bell-Fighting

With a pair of one-pound dumb-bells (they must not be heavier than this for sprinters, and

Bell-fighting.

they need not be so for any type of runner) make a mark on the wall about your chest-level, and

TRAINING EXERCISES

proceed to fight or aim at it with alternate and direct arm deliveries. Work up to top pressure, shooting the arm in and out as fast as you can do, until you tire. The body muscles, back and front, are brought into play and the breathing organs are also exercised.

The "100 up"

Devised and practised by the famous mile-record holder, W. G. George, who found it most

The "100 up."

beneficial for the purpose of keeping the legs in condition for running, by indoor practice. The

"100 upper" toes a mark on the ground and lifts his legs alternately, copying the running movements as closely as possible, coming down to tiptoe on the mark again. A daily course each morning before breakfast by an open window will assist in keeping much of the rust that comes to the joints of the athlete out of practice, and so further his more speedy recovery of form when he comes back to the track. Its benefits are not confined to the active athlete, as a course of this exercise cannot fail to do good to all who take it. The individual must be the best judge as to what suits him best in respect of the pace and duration of the leg movements.

Sprint "Pattering"

To encourage quickness of leg action there is no finer exercise than this. Take the tiniest of strides you are capable of at the utmost limit of your speed. See that you are poised well forward, the arms hung down in front of you and the shoulders worked in the best sprinting manner. The strain is so great that the best of "patterers" will not go much farther than 20 or 30 yards at full pressure. He will only go about half his usual length and be moving his feet so fast that in an action-photograph (or in the accompanying drawing of the exercise) he appears to be hopping lightly

Sprint "pattering" for quick leg action.

off one foot to the other. "Pattering" will sharpen up the most slow-going natures.

The Sprinting Style

The correct action of the sprinter is as illustrated above. Note the loose, drooping down carriage of the arms, with the forearms and hands swung inwards and outwards, pendulum fashion, across the pit of the stomach; the slightly forward pitch of the head and the chest, and the low stride, implying no waste of time or effort, and assured rapidity. One most vital detail may, however, be overlooked (although imprinted there surely enough), and that is the wriggling, rising and falling of the shoulders which govern the arms in the same high proportion that the arms command the legs. This shoulder movement was the real secret of Harry Hutchens' (the fastest runner the world has yet seen) extraordinary speed. His shoulders could be seen bobbing up and down, keeping regular time to the swiftly moving play of his arms.

One may practice the style and gain strength at all the necessary points indoors or outdoors. Every part of the body must be quite loosely held and operated.

GENERAL HEALTH HINTS AND PERSONAL NOTIONS

IT is up to everyone to keep himself or herself in fairly good physical condition. Not all of us can play the popular outdoor games, although there are many entering and well into middle age who can be seen indulging in such robust pursuits as cricket and tennis. It may be depended on that most of them have "never left off." They have preserved some glimpses of their best form and shown a comparatively slight, if gradual, decline from the day that they turned into the fateful thirty-sixth year which divides youth from the true maturity, both in physique and intellect. The outdoor life is, of course, the one to aspire to. Country folk may have it, but the townsman has, usually, to take his glimpses of the fields and charge his lungs with God's fresh air during the interval between the business calls of a stuffy office or workshop. This being so, it is not a matter for wonderment that he soon loses the first blush of youth, often slows down when he reaches the thirties, and becomes an old man before his time. Then the day comes when he repines a lost digestion, a weight of superfluous flesh and a lack-lustre state which can only be cured (so the doctor rightly tells him) by fresh-air and exercise.

The business man and he who leads the sedentary form of studious life are the greatest sufferers. The most healthy are the toilers in the open air. Change their lives and you could guarantee to change their respective states of health.

In between the two extremes come the factory and general indoor workers, whose lot is the hardest of all. Their only chance is to take as much of the air, night and day, as time will permit of their doing. Food is really a secondary consideration, although it ranks high, with cleanliness of body and habit, proper rest and rational clothing. The athlete in training conforms to a simple set of rules which can well be varied to suit all classes—men, women and children alike. He avoids the things which do not agree with his well-being, takes his meals at regular hours, strengthens his limbs and clears lungs and stomach, sleeps his seven or eight hours, going to bed and rising fairly early. He is bright-eyed, clear-headed and at a weight which leaves him master of his own strength and actions.

There may be some virtue in patent medicines,

GENERAL HEALTH HINTS

but the value of the best of these is but slight as compared with what Nature can do for you, with her judicious blending of cleanliness, plain good open-air exercise and living (never forgetting the open window at any time, though taking care of draughts), rest and regularity in everything, with every reasonable precaution set against colds and chills. These common complaints are the beginning of most ailments. " Prevention is better than cure " is a maxim which holds a stronger place in a work on physical training than anywhere else. For exercise improperly taken is the cause of more trouble almost than no exercise at all. So, with a view to inducing the " man in the street," his wife, his sons and daughters to take a little more care of himself, and of themselves, a few general cautions which apply to all who heat the blood, and so put a strain on the heart and muscles by deliberate exercise or unaccustomed exertion, may be found acceptable.

I do not profess to be a health expert nor to command any special knowledge. What I have to say is, I believe, just bound up with simple facts. The skin inhales the air and exhales (to a far greater extent) the fumes and vapours of the body, while the pores are apparently closed. Theirs is, or should be, a continuous function, at its lowest limits in cold weather and at its greatest height in warm weather, or when the blood is overheated by prolonged or very violent efforts. When the blood and the flesh are heated they melt the waste tissues or the fatty products and cause perspiration. The pores of the skin expand and open with the added warmth of the body, and the beads of sweat ooze through.

The skin lets out or keeps in poisonous and superfluous matter according to the habits, the requirements or the understanding of each individual. It provides the only healthy and proper means of reducing weight, either by dry heat (Turkish) or hot vapour (Russian) baths or, far preferably, running, walking or other active exercise in the open air. Indoor sweats are not conducive to good health because they lack in the chief requirement of the body (a greater requirement even than food, rest and clothing)—namely, fresh air. This is best obtained in open spaces, the hillier the better, where grass and trees abound.

There is one drawback, though full of comfort and an absolute necessity, to open-air violent exercise, and that is change of clothing. Whether you are going for a long tramp in the country, rowing, at cricket, tennis, golf even, you should change from your ordinary walking attire and wear the regulation flannels or light knickerbocker suits and good airy clothing while you are engaged in your walk or games. Having finished them, take a shower-bath or sponge-down; in any case have a rub-down with a towel. Avoid anything in the way of food and drink or chilly draughts until you have cooled off, and you feel that the pores of the skin are closed again.

There are thousands of chills contracted every year, mostly between the months of April and October, through neglect of this simple but all-important matter of taking the greatest care of yourself when the pores of the skin are open and you are perspiring. It may be that you came out of a heated room or place of amusement, or started perspiring through overhaste on some muggy day. To go on top of a bus (especially the swift motor buses) in such a condition means a certain chill, the end of which none can foretell. The remedy is to watch yourself closely, and note your surroundings and the effect they have upon you. You can soon shake up the circulation by a brisk walk (the only healthy way) to overcome the cold of the winter months. It is when you are heated that you have to take the greatest care of yourself and cool off gradually. If you are not able to change your clothes take a bath or a rub-down.

These everyday matters apply equally to the athlete in training with all other classes of people. They must come to know that there is nothing more dangerous to their well-being than a cold or a chill; that only by bodily cleanliness can the pores of the skin perform the allotted part they have to play in the upkeep of the body; that exercise is as important as food and rest and fresh air, really more necessary than all these; that a middle-aged man or woman need not necessarily be burdened with fat and incapable of any but the slightest exertion; and that the utmost benefit to the general state, physical and mental, is to be derived from common-sense exercise and habits.

As regards athletic *training*, this is out of the question for boys and youths. They may be taught to carry themselves in the proper way for what they promise to shine at, whether it be sprinting, middle distance, long distance, running, walking even, the jump and hurdles. But they should do no strenuous work at any time. Their frames are unset and they are not physically fitted to take more than gentle exercise. We hear of youthful prodigies in all branches of sport, but it can be depended upon that where any great strain is put upon the organs of a growing youth the result will surely be to his future disadvantage. The old adage of " Early ripe, early rotten," if not sounding well, is pregnant with truth. A boy will take his natural exercise in his games or occupation.

The average man's athletic prime is from twenty-three to thirty-five years of age. In the intervening years he is capable of undergoing the most severe physical tests which his frame can stand. Every man is, of course, a law unto himself, and what might (metaphorically) kill one in the way of exercise would merely be a light pastime for another. The man's own instinct will go far to tell him whether he should be a footballer, cricketer, sculler, rower, boxer, runner, jumper or athletic "strong man." There are really not many who absolutely misplace themselves. Having found his particular athletic hobby, the young man cannot do better than obtain specialist advice, which is, unfortunately, at a discount in England, owing to there being so few inducements for the best trainers to come to the front.

At all events, the growth of the Olympic international rivalry will have achieved its share of good if (as seems probable) it paves the way to a reversion to the " old ways of the old days," when the English foot-runners, jumpers, shot-putters, hammer-throwers and hurdlers had the field to themselves. Things work round in a circle, they say, and if the revolution of the wheel brings us to where we were in the glorious old eighties (of delightful memory), when we had the world's champions in the land (such as we can reproduce again, out of a combination of enthusiasm and knowledge), we shall only come into our own again. The quality of our best instructors and our raw material is unsurpassed. Give them both a real chance (ask men what they *know*, and not depend upon easily won reputations), and the Union Jack will be seen floating up at the top of the winning flagstaff more often than it was at Stockholm, more frequently, too, than at Shepherd's Bush.

No finer subject than the athlete in his prime could be had for one who has lived his life in what some people have described as the " narrow field of athletics." It is something for the Impressionist artist to paint, but not those misshapen, muscle-bound creations of the " Hercules " type and advertising strong men, who are so only to those who do not understand the chief requirements of the shapeliest human bodies. Agility should be as clearly displayed as strength. Those bosses of muscle the weight-lifters are so fond of showing can be developed by the poorest weaklings, *but only at the expense of some other part of their bodies.* The true specimen of the athlete is a level frame with little or no outstanding muscle, when he is in repose, but a rippling play of long, loose, coiling bands

GENERAL HEALTH HINTS

beneath a gleaming skin in the moments of action. Loose and lithe, supply strong, quick of eye and movement, the nervous system in keeping with the muscular, the true athletic ideal means a combination of speed, activity and power such as Nature will best form out of her marvellous self, but which can (but in a minor degree) be developed.

Physical fitness means the subjection of self to the best and cleanest of principles and ideas. Here, in England, we should be at least as forward as they are on the Continent in general training for the young. The only points where we might differ should be the substitution of the rudiments of the primitive outdoor pursuits, such as walking, running and jumping, for the gymnasium. One sound natural exercise is worth the whole bunch of artificial gymnastic culture. There is not the slightest reason why, given encouragement in high quarters, which means all or nothing in the advancement of a new propaganda, we should not have our own English musical drill formed to present the outlines of our leading sports and pastimes.

To those who are prepared to give more than a passing glance at the technical poses shown in various parts of this work, there must come the conviction that, even in running, the matter of correct style has been ignored. Do you ever see the best of the track athletes (and the sprinters, in particular) conform to the true tenets of their art ? The very mechanism of the human body throws the searchlight of the student upon the keys which must be touched to put its bearings into the best working order. But running is such a common action—everybody runs, more or less—that its very claims to be regarded for what it is, a marvellous combination of the nervous and muscular forces, added to the fluent working of the joints below and all the parts above, are overlooked. If it were not so, we should have a far superior class of runner at every distance.

Humour the young, teach them the outlines of style and urge upon them the folly of making any real effort until they have turned the precarious age of twenty-one years. Then, in the flower of their vitality, they may come (and then only by degrees) to bring out the best that is in them. If a track athlete does not lose entire touch of his especial department, whether this be running, walking, jumping, hurdling, the shot or hammer, he will keep going for, perhaps, a dozen years and be able to find his best form with a sufficient preparation. To do this, he should either get out in the roads or the track once or twice a week all the year round. There are indoor exercises, such as are set out in other sections of this book, which will nearly suffice to the same purpose in

GENERAL HEALTH HINTS

very inclement weather. Retention of form is, in this way, rendered comparatively easy. By contrast, the disappointments which come with the loss of speed or ability after many months out of harness make the trouble one has taken to keep moving well worth the while.

Once the average amateur athlete nears the thirties, he gets the notion into his head that it is time he should retire. The thought of the burden of veteranship seems to weigh too heavily upon him. It is, however, quite a mistaken feeling. As a matter of fact, a hale, hearty man can go on until he is forty, although he will be losing in fire and dash in the last three or four years. By way of a counterbalance he should be gifted with greater stamina. This is again the natural order of things. Many sprint-runners (the long-limbed kind particularly) have lost their speed on turning into the thirties, to suddenly discover that they can go on to run quite a decent half-mile. A little thought will again tell how this change is brought about. Unable to fairly extend himself at the short distance as he used to do, the sprinter retains his action while having said " good-bye for ever " to his former light, lively striding. If he examines his footprints he will find that he is stretching himself out much farther than he used to when sprinting at his best, in the manner of the middle-distance men. And, doing so, he can run farther and stronger than he thought he would ever be able to do, simply because his best pace is nothing like what it was, although he has the same inner vitality, but less pliant muscles and joints.

If the many athletes who " retire " and pass out of active track life at or before thirty years of age were to keep going, their development into more pronounced stayers than they were suspected to be would set a new fashion. This would take the form of seeing more young middle-aged, full middle-aged, old and very old men careering about the few athletic tracks left to most of our cities. If the average man came to understand the great health value of gentle natural exercise in the open air, and the outstanding merits of running and walking (easily but regularly taken), followed by the tub or shower and rub-down, there would be fewer ailing and bewailing loss of shape and the resultant evils. I may hardly be believed if I state that the several septuagenarians I have known to continue their track exercise up to the allotted span of human life have had the clean, ruddy-hued skin of a child, and with eyes as clear and bright.

If not exactly the conqueror of all ills that may befall the flesh, running and walking in the open air for the middle-aged and old, with proper treatment in the dressing-room, and a set of

GENERAL HEALTH HINTS 245

sensible, easy exercises, would reduce the toll of suffering and incapacity as no other form of treatment can hope to do. All other panaceas are as the molehill to the mountain. Home exercises are better than none at all, if quite of a makeshift kind. But they are liable to be harmful unless conducted in a fresh atmosphere —that is to say, where windows and doors are and have been open. A brisk jog over the fields or a nice walk in the lanes or parks before breakfast will be more effectual as a remedy to the accumulating courses of ill health than anything else. A hale, hearty man may go on through the forties, the fifties and the sixties, doing his bit of exercise by keeping his legs going, and his body swaying. In the writer's list of acquaintances is an old man of seventy years of age who can run his 100 yards in 14 seconds; what is more he prefers 150 yards—he runs on so strongly—to the hundred. He is not an exception by any means, as there is a gay seventy-three-year-older somewhere in the north of England, who won an open sprint handicap last year (1912) and immediately threw out a challenge to run anyone in the world, of seventy years or over, a match at 60 yards.

There was the pathetic case, just over twelve months ago, of a former sprint champion of London (one David Isaacs), who succumbed to the effects of an operation at one of the big hospitals. The day before he was taken there, he had actually given a runner thirty-five years his junior a yard start in a sprint handicap heat and only been beaten by a bare few inches. In his sixty-seventh year, he was then a model of the truest physical culture. No bosses of muscles (the sure sign of slowness as well as of strength) anywhere, but a certain lithe muscular system, reminding one of the whippet or greyhound. With skin as clear as a child and a suppleness of limb which was really astonishing to behold, this relic of a former glory stood as an example of what true physical training, natural and therefore unforced, can achieve in one near the end of his life. He withstood a most painful and prolonged surgical operation, but in the days of an especially sunless January (the sun *is* the life !) he gradually sunk where few would have lasted out at all under the twofold strain of the surgeon's friendly knife and anæsthetics.

Isaacs was the greatest student of foot-racing matters that the professional section will, probably, ever know. He was a walking encyclopædia of athletic lore and a very practical exemplar on the track, and when surveying, watch in hand, the performances of others there. In his rough way he knew the value of correct form. As a judge of a handicap he certainly had no superior and, it may be, no equal. But he was not the stamp of man to impart his knowledge to others. Educated in a school which had secrecy as its chief subject, this remarkable old man kept to himself and stored in his mind the dictionary of hard facts he had gleaned in his half-century's connexion with foot-running. He had seen the days when there was no sport more popular, and the other side of the picture—when no other pastime was so poor as to do it reverence. He marks the passing of an old era, and, it is to be hoped, the coming of a new and (shall we say) better one.

If the introduction of this old-time character of the running track may not seem to be entirely in place, the excuse must be the writer's predilection for the first glimpse that he had of track and field sports, which led to his observance of systematic method. It led to an acquaintance with the stars of the path, and, notably, the sprint-running experts, who were, at the close of the seventies, in the heyday of their popularity. They were " kept " and trained for years together, before the eventful day came round that found them backed to win many thousands of pounds and called upon to justify their employer's judgment, care and patience. Runners came from all parts of the world to take part in these " pedestrian Derbys." Now and again an American or a Canadian came out on top; but these were fleeting exceptions to the general rule that England was the home of all the great runners, sprinters and distance-men alike.

Now, " to point a moral and adorn the tale," it has to be told that the professionals maintained British supremacy in foot-racing until their hold on the public—foolishly and deservedly lost—not by the runners themselves, but by the men who controlled their doings—waned. Then, with the growing strength of genuine amateur athletics (not its subsequent hybrid active and legislative condition), came a period of an improved class of athlete, morally and capably. Under the guidance of the professionals, the amateurs developed faster times. And it is safe to say that, in the eighties, we could much more than hold our own with either set, professionals or amateurs, against the world. The names of Harry Hutchens (the sprint phenomenon), W. G. George (of mile record fame), and the peerless Sheffielder, George Littlewood (able to lower all previous bests, from one hour to days, either walking or running), stood out alone, while among the amateurs there were the black sprinter, A. Wharton, the eastern shires Herculean sprinter and quarter-miler, C. G. Wood, the 'varsity quarter and half milers, H. C. L. Tindall and F. J. K. Cross (who also won the mile, although this was above the length of his best distance), W. G. George (until he turned to professionalism), W. Snook (from 1 to 10 miles), Sid Thomas (4 to 10 miles), and a host of others. We have had good men since, but none better than they; nor has the quality been in such abundance, although the recorded times mostly favour those who followed them, because of the circumstances which carried the annual championship meetings all over the country, and the difficulty of setting one set of conditions against another.

Good as the amateur has often proved himself to be, there is not the slightest doubt that he would have been far better had he adopted the technique of the professional, such as is done in cricket, football, rowing, boxing, billiards and in all games of skill. For example, both Wharton and W. G. George were improved greatly by a professional regime. Afterwards, in the passing craze of the " new professionalism " of the nineties, such lights of the amateur world as A. R. Downer, E. C. Bredin, F. E. Bacon and H. Watkins did not go back, and one, at least, of them improved in no small measure. Since that short relapse to what has been described as the " methods of barbarism," we have really great runners in Shrubb, and Lieutenant W. Halswelle, E. R. Voigt, several of the 'varsity men (who have, unfortunately, not been seen without their own select games) and the present-day celebrities, the Oxonian, A. N. S. Jackson (the miler) and that dapper little sprinter, W. R. Applegarth, who has, certainly, trained on to produce a rate of speed such as has not been at the command of a sprinter since the old professional ascendancy of thirty years ago. All that he needed was to come under the supervision of one who could trace those several little faults of his, the smoothing down of which has meant so much to him.

There is not the slightest attempt being made here to belittle the amateur athlete and to glorify the professional. That would be as wrong as it is silly. Professional or amateur, all came out of the same basket. But with the extra attention bestowed upon the rearing of the better-class amateur athlete; his longer delay in entering the workaday world; his presumably higher intelligence and other advantages, should fashion him to be the better man. Some of these theories work out true, as a visit to that splendid annual sports carnival at Queen's Club, West Kensington, where the master athletes of the two great English seats of learning are pitted one against the other, shows. The running achievements of some of the winners, who are obviously quite untaught, simply bewilder one. We had thought in the

GENERAL HEALTH HINTS

old days that no such a half-miler as W. Williams of Sunderland (who could "do" 1 minute 50 seconds and also run a "quarter" in 48 seconds—and be some 2 seconds behind Hutchens, according to calculations, at that) would ever be seen again. But when you see comparative novices "doing" 1 minute 55 seconds and 1 minute 56 seconds for their half-miles in cold, howling winds and on a heavy, soddened track, you view things in a newer, clearer light, or should do so.

Distance-men, jumpers and hurdlers of exceptional calibre keep cropping up in the inter-university sports. They go to confirm the impression that there is a wealth of talent among the well-bred youth of the country. Where the leanness of the land is exposed is in the sprints. Now and again there is a fast quarter-mile, but never any really good sprinting, simply because there is no sprint coach (who has gone into its many details and is able to show the inner side of this most delicate branch of track athletics) now practising in "fashionable circles." It is here that the Americans (with not a little to learn themselves of fast running) supplement their vast superiority in the field events, where ordered strength and much practice, under careful tuition, spells success.

In England, here, we have such an abundance of raw material as no other country possesses. Were it possible to-day, even in our neglected state, to put teams of 200 men, drawn from each country, into competition at all running distances, jumps and field games, I don't doubt that we should easily head the list. An intelligent system of training would assuredly give us the individual as well as the team championships. The man who will come along and set the athletic house in order will deserve well of his country. To fire the imagination of the younger generation to again take the old-time interest in the track and field sports, for their own personal welfare as well as for a fitter race and enhanced national prestige, would be doing a greater and better work than the founding of libraries or the endowment of charities. He would, too, deserve (and surely receive) a suitable reward in the shape of the appreciation of those who can differentiate between mere ostentation and a true desire to do some good in the world.

Before closing these rambling impressions of what might and could be, the matter of suitable dress may well be touched upon. It is a complex subject. The advocates of woollen clothing have been many and distinguished. To me, however, they have seemed to always provide

GENERAL HEALTH HINTS

against the most rigorous weather, leaving the warm, muggy and mild days to care for themselves. In England here, with the young people, it is either one extreme or the other, cuddled up in thick underclothing the winter through, to suddenly burst forth from their bondage and often discard all but absolutely necessary outer raiment during the fleeting summertide. This is, of course, unwise, equally with the overburdening and artificial warming of the system in the colder months of the year. The great thing is to strike the happy medium between the two extremes. Personally, I flatter myself that I have long ago succeeded in doing so. All the year round next to my skin I wear a little openwork cotton vest. It is a network in which the cavities occupy much more space than the material. In the summer these little vests (they cost me $6\frac{1}{2}$d. each) are delightfully cool; in the winter they give (to me) all possible warmth. More than this, I contend they enable me to lead a natural life by allowing the exhalations from the pores of the skin to be carried off and the air to reach and refresh them. Another point, I do not wear under-drawers and only the plainest of knitted woollen socks.

Some people have told me that I am a crank, others that this light way of dressing may suit me, where it might do harm to most. Of the first imputation I am not the best judge; and of the second, I have to admit there is reason in such a contention. But of this I am certain, that the robust man or woman in the prime of life, well nourished and taking a reasonable amount of exercise, needs little more underclothing than I do. I may have a greater vitality than most (and with all due respect to everybody else, I hope, as I believe, that this is so) owing to a natural legacy and a lifelong connexion with all manner of field sports. All the best, hardiest and most resolute athletes I have known were those who wore just a linen shirt and nothing else under their outer clothes. Granted that they were the right stamp, hewn out by nature, the fact remains that they could easily have been spoiled by a fulsome application of woollen and flannel clothing on their bodies. For people of low vitality, who take little exercise, warm underclothing is indispensable. But they are hothouse plants that shrivel up when the fresh, pure air of the heavens touches them. And I am sorry to say that there are tens of thousands of our city youths and young men, with lungs and tonsils charged with the poisonous fumes of cheap cigarettes and vitiated air, who are of this unhealthy stamp.

Whether conscription be good or bad for this Old England of ours it is not for me to decide. But I would support any such measure to the best of my ability were I sure that with it would come a new and enforced code of health rules. These should be framed to drive all the young people, capable of using their limbs and their senses, into the beautiful parks and open spaces which have—thanks be to common-sense—been secured for the people in every quarter of the kingdom. Look at the wonderful expanse of Hyde Park! What might not be done with it as a centre of sensible physical recreation for the rising generations? Some of the public money that is being squandered on educational subjects for the mind, and which will not be of the slightest service to one in a thousand, might well be directed to a higher and better cause. To have travelled through the heart of the Continent is to feel a sense of shame that our own youngsters, who come of the finest stock the world will ever know, are not given the same health opportunities as those of other and poorer countries. There is too much counting-the-cost as regards personal interests and jealous rivalries instead of there being that harmonious surrendering of the pocket to the physical welfare of those who have to carry on the race at the wrong end of the ladder.

One hears much of breathing exercises. In certain circumstances they have their special value. But to ordinary persons, or to the athlete taking plenty of walking (*not* strolling), running, cricket, tennis, golf, etc., in the open air, they are not a necessity. A good striding walk with your head up and your chest out will nicely open the lungs. For a real " pipe-opener," however, running is the thing, if only a mere trot. You will soon find out whether you are thick or clear in the wind, too, at golf, to say nothing of the more exacting calls of cricket or tennis. You will get all the breathing exercises you require in this manner, while buoying up the body with invigorating calls upon it. The deep inflations made to order should mostly be reserved for those who do not or cannot take other open-air recreation. The best breathing exercises are those made through the opened mouth and taken, of course, out-doors. When the sun is shining, or the ozone of the sea or the hills is available, there can be no doubt of the good that deep breathing will do for everyone.

As to smoking and the drinking of alcoholic liquors, they are acquired habits, harmful to most but beneficial to some. Many an athlete

GENERAL HEALTH HINTS 257

in training finds pleasure in a cigarette after a meal. It may aid his digestion, so long as he does not inhale the smoke. But the real topnotchers leave smoking severely alone. Their instinct tells them that it is neither good for the breathing organs nor the nerves. Good beer, brewed of malt and hops, has a decided value as a food. There is no better tonic than a tankard of genuine ale and nothing more sustaining than a glass of stout. Moderation is the chief thing. Those who can do without either have the gratification of knowing that they can take consolation in the seasonable fruits and vegetables and Nature's greatest liquid food—milk.

With regard to food, too much meat-eating is not good. Mutton is decidedly better for the athlete (and for the great majority of people) than beef; and fresh meat is infinitely better than any which has been pickled or preserved. Pork and veal (especially) cannot be recommended. A good beef or mutton stew will work wonders with a lowered temperature or depressed nerves. Above all milk-porridge (made of oatmeal taking its full hour to cook) will build up the nervous system as nothing else can do. Poultry and game are most acceptable as a change. The athlete in training requires plenty of changes. The old-fashioned notion that only dry toast and raw steak, washed down with beer, was of any service to him, has long ago been exploded. Meat-pies and meat-puddings may be rather rich, heavy fare for some, but quite suitable to the greater number. Potatoes, butter, cheese and bread (well-baked, stale and of a crispy crust) are indispensable. Bacon (as obtained in the big cities) is a fallacy; fresh eggs are wonderfully nourishing to nine out of ten, but almost a deadly poison to the tenth person; good fresh or dried (dried, not pickled) fish will be to the taste and suit all but a select few whose systems cannot assimilate anything taken out of the sea; last, but not least, the after-pudding of milky tapioca, sago, rice, semolina or bread and butter, and the plain suet puddings or those with the added luxury of sultanas or currants as presenting easily digested and most nourishing foodstuffs.

The bath that is most neglected of any is the easiest and cheapest to take. I mean the air and sun bath. For anyone, and for the athlete in training more than all others, the purifying of the system by God's fresh air and sun rays means nothing short of the induction of the real elixir of life. With the pores of the skin cleansed of their natural grease by the water-bath after exercise, an hour or so's exposure of the naked body to the sunlight is a precious

GENERAL HEALTH HINTS 259

thing. Never hurry to get your clothes on during the sunny, high-temperatured days of spring, summer and autumn. Let the body draw in the electrical atoms which float amidst those transmitted beams of glowing heat. Remember that we were originally destined to lead the outdoor life bereft of clothing. The air and sun bath stands for a fleeting return to the first natural state.

Without any desire to glorify the athlete beyond his limits, that most truthful maxim, "the survival of the fittest," will always rise up invincibly before the man who attempts to write or speak on health or training matters. It is pregnant with common-sense. Eminently an English phrase, one feels it would gain greater force were it applied to the highest uses in this country. For instance, there is our "splendidly equipped little army," which I (for one) patriotically wish may be all as near to that stage of perfection as is claimed for it by our own military experts. Comparatively, and man for man, there may be that measure of superiority generally admitted over the Continental conscript armies. This may mean much or not so very much. In the first place, every soldier should be developed to the utmost of his abilities as a pedestrian athlete. Speed and endurance are (according to my own observations) the very soul of modern military undertakings, now that the scouting is done from high up among the clouds. Changes of position will now be made (more than ever) under the cloak of night.

If these statements are admitted (and who will deny their sober truth?), why are the foot soldiers taught to walk or march in an unnatural and retarding style? A soldier should be a fighting man trained to that great end, not to be so ordered in his movements as to mainly look imposing on parade or at state ceremonials. *To keep his shoulders stiff and his arms working in semi-rigid, right-angled strokes from the elbow* is both a waste of energy and pace. With a less effort the marching foot soldier can cover several extra inches at each stride and walk in the manner that his Maker intended him to do. Loose, supple motions, with every part of the body swinging rhythmically, will mean fewer men falling out, not so severe a strain upon the heart and therefore greater recuperative powers. Are not these prime qualities in the fighting man?

I have not the exact terms of the quotation by me, but I believe I am correct in saying that Napoleon (surely *the* authority on the mechanism of war!) declared that a good marcher was of greater value to an army than a crack shot.

GENERAL HEALTH HINTS 261

The more one looks into this assertion the more clearly is its meaning and correctness realized. The man who can *get to the tactical points* is the better soldier. All the daredevil courage, steadiness and fine shooting in the world will not avail the soldier unable to keep pace with the changing positions of his corps. He is an encumbrance unless tied down to the trenches, a third or fourth class fighting instrument. In modern warfare only the really first-class men are likely to be of service.

As an incentive to every soldier in the British army to become a pattern of soldiering efficiency and an example to all ranks, it is the opinion of the writer that a *Corps d'Élite*, composed only of men able to walk seven miles or over per hour (in athletic costume on the walking track or road), would set up a standard of competitiveness the results of which would be felt on every side. From being able to perform this good, but not excessively fast, walking, this preliminary qualification would bring with it some equally good, if not better, proportionate achievements in full service marching order. But the walking must be of the loose, swaying shoulders and hips kind, with the rifle slung over the shoulder, the hands allowed free play across the groin, taught by competent instructors. The effect, with its suggestion of pace and ease, would be far more pleasing to the eye than the cast-iron marching incorrectly supposed to be the acme of military form and which the men cannot shake off (especially the shoulder and arm crudities) even when they would be allowed to do so. Here is a direction for the energies of some soldier-athlete.

Finale

It will doubtless be noticed that the special field games of the pole-vault, discus and javelin throwing, along with that fine sport, cross-country running, are not included in this book. There is no attempt made to underrate their importance or rob them of their proper place amongst current athletics. The writer is, however, diffident of touching subjects with which he has had so little practical acquaintance; and it would not be fair to his readers for him to paraphrase the works of others or advance second-hand opinions. So he considers the only honest way out of a difficulty is to "own up" to his deficiencies and beg the indulgence of those who do him the honour to take notice of his opinions and theories in other athletic directions.

INDEX

APPLEGARTH, W. R., 250

BACON, F. E., 249
Bredin, E. C., 249

GEORGE, W. G., 74, 248

HALF-MILE RACE, the, 66-69; schedule times of, 69
Hammer-throwing, 185-187; standards of, 187
Health hints and personal notions, general, 233-262; fitness, 233-235; natural exercises, 241-242; age, 243-249; present-day athletes, 249, 251
High jump, the, 173-176; standards of, 176
Hop, step and jump, 177-180
Hurdles, the, 161-168; evolution of style of, 161-166

ISAACS, David, 245-247

JACKSON, A. N. S., 250

LITTLEWOOD, George, 248
Long jump, the, 169-172; standards of, 172

ONE-MILE RACE, the, 70-75; champions of the, 70; preparation, 72-75; schedule, times of, 75

PUTTING THE SHOT, 181-184; standards of, 184

QUARTER-MILE RACE, the, 59-65; preparation, 62-64; schedule times of, 65

RUNNING AND WALKING, the rudiments of, 1-7
Running, long-distance, 76,-83 schedule of times of, 83
Running, Marathon, 84-117; preparations, 85-87; medicine, 87-88; foot pickle, 88; shoes and socks, 89-94; daily routine, 94-95; duration of training, 95-99; preliminary training, 99-101; schedule of times of, 102; what to do when fit, 102-105; long walks, 105, 106; diet, 107-108; what to wear, 110-111; on the day of race, 111-113; champions of, 113-115

SHOES, 188-194; differing patterns for various distances, 188-189; length and placing of spikes, 189-194
Shrubb, 249
Snook, W., 249
Sprint-running, 9-53; sprinters' length, 30; action, 13-19; striding, 20-21; on the track, 22-26; preparation, 26-40; schedule of average times by various classes of, 39; starting, 40-53; longer, 54-58; schedule times of long, 58
Starting, 195-199; style, 196; the starter, 197-199
Stride measuring and tracing, 216-221; diagram of, 217

TACTICS, Track. *See* Track Tactics
Timing or watch-holding, 200-211; table for the use of making handicaps, 202; watch-holding "impressions," 207-211
Tindall, H. C. L., 248

Track Tactics, 118-134; examples of, 121-131; diagrams of, 126
Track, care of the, 212-215
Training exercises, 223-232; arm and shoulder swing, 223-224; leg-dance, 224-225; skipping, 225-226; raising and stretching, 226-227; bell-fighting, 228-229; sprint "pattering," 230-231; the sprinting style, 231-232
Training methods, true, 135-151; the trainer, 135-138; care of feet, 138-139; the massage, 140-141; hurts, 146-148; baths and sweating, 141-145

Training section, introduction to, 222

VOIGT, E. R., 249

WALKING AND RUNNING, rudiments of, 1-7
Walking, track and road, 152-160; schedule times of, 159; preparation; 159-160
Watkins, H., 249
Wharton, A., 200
Williams, W., 251
Wood, C. G., 250

MARCH, 1923

A SELECTION FROM

MESSRS. METHUEN'S PUBLICATIONS

This Catalogue contains only a selection of the more important books published by Messrs. Methuen. A complete catalogue of their publications may be obtained on application.

Armstrong (W. W.). THE ART OF CRICKET. *Cr. 8vo.* 6s. *net.*
Bain (F. W.).—
A DIGIT OF THE MOON: A Hindoo Love Story. THE DESCENT OF THE SUN: A Cycle of Birth. A HEIFER OF THE DAWN. IN THE GREAT GOD'S HAIR. A DRAUGHT OF THE BLUE. AN ESSENCE OF THE DUSK. AN INCARNATION OF THE SNOW. A MINE OF FAULTS. THE ASHES OF A GOD. BUBBLES OF THE FOAM. A SYRUP OF THE BEES. THE LIVERY OF EVE. THE SUBSTANCE OF A DREAM. *All Fcap. 8vo.* 5s. *net.* AN ECHO OF THE SPHERES. *Wide Demy.* 12s. 6d. *net.*
Baker (C. H. Collins). CROME. Illustrated. *Quarto.* £5 5s. *net.*
Balfour (Sir Graham). THE LIFE OF ROBERT LOUIS STEVENSON. *Twentieth Edition. In one Volume. Cr. 8vo. Buckram.* 7s. 6d. *net.*
Bateman (H. M.). A BOOK OF DRAWINGS. *Fifth Edition. Royal 4to.* 10s. 6d. *net.*
MORE DRAWINGS. *Second Edition. Royal 4to.* 10s. 6d. *net.*
SUBURBIA. *Demy 4to.* 6s. *net.*
Belloc (H.)—
PARIS, 8s. 6d. *net.* HILLS AND THE SEA, 6s. *net.* ON NOTHING AND KINDRED SUBJECTS, 6s. *net.* ON EVERYTHING, 6s. *net.* ON SOMETHING, 6s *net.* FIRST AND LAST, 6s. *net.* THIS AND THAT AND THE OTHER, 6s. *net.* MARIE ANTOINETTE, 18s. *net.* ON. *Fcap. 8vo.* 6s. *net.* THE PYRENEES. *Cr. 8vo.* 8s. 6d. *net.*
Blackmore (S. Powell). LAWN TENNIS UP-TO-DATE. Illustrated. *Demy 8vo.* 12s. 6d. *net.*
Carpenter (G. H.). INSECT TRANSFORMATION. *Demy 8vo.* 12s. 6d. *net.*
Chandler (Arthur), D.D., late Lord Bishop of Bloemfontein—
ARA CŒLI: An Essay in Mystical Theology, 5s. *net.* FAITH AND EXPERIENCE, 5s. *net.* THE CULT OF THE PASSING MOMENT, 6s. *net.* THE ENGLISH CHURCH AND REUNION, 5s. *net.* SCALA MUNDI, 4s. 6d. *net.*
Chesterton (G. K.)—
THE BALLAD OF THE WHITE HORSE. ALL THINGS CONSIDERED. TREMENDOUS TRIFLES. ALARMS AND DISCURSIONS. A MISCELLANY OF MEN. THE USES OF DIVERSITY. *All Fcap. 8vo.* 6s. *net.* WINE, WATER, AND SONG. *Fcap. 8vo.* 1s. 6d. *net.*

Clark (Norman). HOW TO BOX. Illustrated. *Cr. 8vo.* 7s. 6d. *net.*
Clutton-Brock (A.). WHAT IS THE KINGDOM OF HEAVEN? *Fifth Edition. Fcap. 8vo.* 5s. *net.*
ESSAYS ON ART. *Second Edition. Fcap. 8vo.* 5s. *net.*
ESSAYS ON BOOKS. *Third Edition. Fcap. 8vo.* 6s. *net.*
MORE ESSAYS ON BOOKS. *Fcap. 8vo.* 6s. *net.*
SHAKESPEARE'S HAMLET. *Fcap. 8vo.* 5s. *net.*
SHELLEY: THE MAN AND THE POET. *Fcap 8vo.* 7s. 6d. *net.*
Conrad (Joseph). THE MIRROR OF THE SEA: Memories and Impressions. *Fourth Edition. Fcap. 8vo.* 6s. *net.*
Drever (James). THE PSYCHOLOGY OF EVERYDAY LIFE. *Third Edition. Cr. 8vo.* 6s. *net.*
THE PSYCHOLOGY OF INDUSTRY. *Cr. 8vo.* 5s. *net.*
Einstein (A.). RELATIVITY: THE SPECIAL AND THE GENERAL THEORY. Translated by ROBERT W. LAWSON. *Seventh Edition. Cr. 8vo.* 5s. *net.*
SIDELIGHTS ON RELATIVITY. Two Lectures by ALBERT EINSTEIN. *Cr. 8vo.* 3s. 6d. *net.*
THE MEANING OF RELATIVITY. *Cr. 8vo.* 5s. *net.*
  Other Books on the **Einstein Theory.**
SPACE—TIME—MATTER. By HERMANN WEYL. *Demy 8vo.* 18s. *net.*
EINSTEIN THE SEARCHER: HIS WORK EXPLAINED IN DIALOGUES WITH EINSTEIN. By ALEXANDER MOSZKOWSKI. *Demy 8vo.* 12s. 6d. *net.*
AN INTRODUCTION TO THE THEORY OF RELATIVITY. By LYNDON BOLTON. *Second Edition. Cr. 8vo.* 5s. *net.*
RELATIVITY AND GRAVITATION. By Various Writers. Edited by J. MALCOLM BIRD. *Cr. 8vo.* 8s. 6d. *net.*
RELATIVITY AND THE UNIVERSE. By Dr. HARRY SCHMIDT. *Second Edition. Cr. 8vo.* 5s. *net.*
THE IDEAS OF EINSTEIN'S THEORY. By J. H. THIRRING. *Cr. 8vo.* 5s. *net.*
RELATIVITY FOR ALL. By HERBERT DINGLE. *Third Edition. Fcap. 8vo.* 2s. *net.*
Evans (Joan). ENGLISH JEWELLERY. *Royal 4to.* £2 12s. 6d. *net.*

Messrs. Methuen's Publications

"Fougasse." A GALLERY OF GAMES. *Fcap. 4to.* 3s. 6d. net.
DRAWN AT A VENTURE. *Royal 4to.* 10s. 6d. net.
Freundlich (Dr. Herbert). COLLOID AND CAPILLARY CHEMISTRY. *Demy 8vo.* 36s. net.
Fyleman (Rose). FAIRIES AND CHIMNEYS. *Fcap. 8vo. Fourteenth Edition.* 3s. 6d. net.
THE FAIRY GREEN. *Seventh Edition. Fcap. 8vo.* 3s. 6d. net.
THE FAIRY FLUTE. *Third Edition. Fcap. 8vo.* 3s. 6d. net.
THE RAINBOW CAT AND OTHER STORIES. *Fcap. 8vo.* 3s. 6d. net.
Gibbins (H. de B.). INDUSTRY IN ENGLAND: HISTORICAL OUTLINES. With Maps and Plans. *Tenth Edition. Demy 8vo..* 12s. 6d. net.
THE INDUSTRIAL HISTORY OF ENGLAND. With 5 Maps and a Plan. *Twenty-seventh Edition. Cr. 8vo.* 5s.
Gibbon (Edward). THE DECLINE AND FALL OF THE ROMAN EMPIRE. Edited, with Notes, Appendices, and Maps, by J. B. Bury. *Seven Volumes. Demy 8vo.* Illustrated. *Each* 12s. 6d. net. Also *in Seven Volumes.* Unillustrated. *Cr. 8vo. Each* 7s. 6d. net.
Glover (T. R.).—
The Conflict of Religions in the Early Roman Empire, 10s. 6d. net. Poets and Puritans, 10s. 6d. net. From Pericles to Philip, 10s. 6d. net. Virgil, 10s. 6d. net. The Christian Tradition and its Verification (The Angus Lecture for 1912). 6s. net.
Grahame (Kenneth). THE WIND IN THE WILLOWS. *Twelfth Edition. Cr. 8vo.* 7s. 6d. net.
Also small 4to. 10s. 6d. net. Illustrated by Nancy Barnhart.
Hall (H. R.). THE ANCIENT HISTORY OF THE NEAR EAST FROM THE EARLIEST TIMES TO THE BATTLE OF SALAMIS. Illustrated. *Fifth Edition. Demy 8vo.* 21s. net.
Holdsworth (W. S.). A HISTORY OF ENGLISH LAW. *Seven Volumes. Demy 8vo. Each* 25s. net.
Inge (W. R.). CHRISTIAN MYSTICISM. (The Bampton Lectures of 1899.) *Fifth Edition. Cr. 8vo.* 7s. 6d. net.
Jenks (E.). AN OUTLINE OF ENGLISH LOCAL GOVERNMENT. *Fifth Edition. Cr. 8vo.* 5s. net.
A SHORT HISTORY OF ENGLISH LAW: From the Earliest Times to the End of the Year 1911. *Second Edition. Demy 8vo.* 12s. 6d. net.
Julian (Lady) of Norwich. REVELATIONS OF DIVINE LOVE. Edited by Grace Warrack. *Seventh Edition. Cr. 8vo.* 5s. net.
Keats (John). POEMS. Edited, with Introduction and Notes, by E. de Selincourt. With a Frontispiece in Photogravure. *Fourth Edition. Demy 8vo.* 12s. 6d. net.
Kidd (Benjamin). THE SCIENCE OF POWER. *Ninth Edition. Cr. 8vo.* 7s. 6d. net.
SOCIAL EVOLUTION. *Demy 8vo.* 8s. 6d. net.
A PHILOSOPHER WITH NATURE. *Second Edition. Cr. 8vo.* 6s. net.
Kipling (Rudyard). BARRACK-ROOM BALLADS. 228th Thousand. *Cr. 8vo.* Buckram, 7s. 6d. net. Also *Fcap. 8vo.* Cloth, 6s. net; leather, 7s. 6d. net.
Also a Service Edition. *Two Volumes. Square Fcap. 8vo. Each* 3s. net.
THE SEVEN SEAS. 161st Thousand. *Cr. 8vo.* Buckram, 7s. 6d. net. Also *Fcap. 8vo.* Cloth, 6s. net; leather, 7s. 6d. net.
Also a Service Edition. *Two Volumes. Square Fcap. 8vo. Each* 3s. net.
THE FIVE NATIONS. 129th Thousand. *Cr. 8vo.* Buckram, 7s. 6d. net. Also *Fcap. 8vo.* Cloth, 6s. net; leather, 7s. 6d. net.
Also a Service Edition. *Two Volumes. Square Fcap. 8vo. Each* 3s. net.
DEPARTMENTAL DITTIES. 103rd Thousand. *Cr. 8vo.* Buckram, 7s. 6d. net. Also *Fcap. 8vo.* Cloth, 6s. net; leather, 7s. 6d. net.
Also a Service Edition. *Two Volumes. Square Fcap. 8vo. Each* 3s. net.
THE YEARS BETWEEN. 95th Thousand. *Cr. 8vo.* Buckram, 7s. 6d. net. *Fcap. 8vo.* Cloth, 6s. net; leather, 7s. 6d. net.
Also a Service Edition. *Two Volumes. Square Fcap. 8vo. Each* 3s. net.
A KIPLING ANTHOLOGY—VERSE. *Fcap. 8vo.* cloth, 6s. net. Leather, 7s. 6d. net.
TWENTY POEMS FROM RUDYARD KIPLING. 313th Thousand. *Fcap. 8vo.* 1s. net.
Knox (E. V. G.). ('Evoe' of *Punch*.) PARODIES REGAINED. Illustrated by George Morrow. *Fcap. 8vo.* 4s. 6d. net.
THESE LIBERTIES. *Fcap. 8vo.* 4s. 6d. net.
Lamb (Charles and Mary). THE COMPLETE WORKS. Edited by E. V. Lucas. *A New and Revised Edition in Six Volumes.* With Frontispieces. *Fcap. 8vo. Each* 6s. net.
The volumes are:—
I. Miscellaneous Prose. II. Elia and the Last Essay of Elia. III. Books for Children. IV. Plays and Poems. V. and VI. Letters.
Lankester (Sir Ray). SCIENCE FROM AN EASY CHAIR. Illustrated. *Thirteenth Edition. Cr. 8vo.* 7s. 6d. net.
SCIENCE FROM AN EASY CHAIR. *Second Series.* Illustrated. *Third Edition. Cr. 8vo.* 7s. 6d. net.
DIVERSIONS OF A NATURALIST. Illustrated. *Third Edition. Cr. 8vo.* 7s. 6d. net.

Messrs. Methuen's Publications

SECRETS OF EARTH AND SEA. *Cr. 8vo. 8s. 6d. net.*
GREAT AND SMALL THINGS. Illustrated. *Cr. 8vo. 7s. 6d. net.*
Lescarboura (A. C.) RADIO FOR EVERYBODY. Illustrated. *Cr. 8vo. 7s. 6d. net.*
Lodge (Sir Oliver). MAN AND THE UNIVERSE. *Ninth Edition. Cr. 8vo. 7s. 6d. net.*
THE SURVIVAL OF MAN: A STUDY IN UNRECOGNIZED HUMAN FACULTY. *Seventh Edition. Cr. 8vo. 7s. 6d. net.*
MODERN PROBLEMS. *Cr. 8vo. 7s. 6d. net.*
RAYMOND; OR LIFE AND DEATH. Illustrated. *Twelfth Edition. Demy 8vo. 10s. 6d. net.*
RAYMOND REVISED. (Abbreviated edition). *Cr. 8vo. 6s. net.*
Loring (F. H.). ATOMIC THEORIES. *Second Edition. Demy 8vo. 12s. 6d. net.*
Lucas (E. V.)—
THE LIFE OF CHARLES LAMB, 2 vols., 21s. net. A WANDERER IN HOLLAND, 10s. 6d. net. A WANDERER IN LONDON, 10s. 6d. net. LONDON REVISITED, 10s. 6d. net. A WANDERER IN PARIS, 10s. 6d. net and 6s. net. A WANDERER IN FLORENCE, 10s. 6d. net. A WANDERER IN VENICE, 10s. 6d. net. THE OPEN ROAD: A Little Book for Wayfarers, 6s. 6d. net. THE FRIENDLY TOWN: A Little Book for the Urbane, 6s. net. FIRESIDE AND SUNSHINE, 6s. net. CHARACTER AND COMEDY, 6s. net. THE GENTLEST ART: A Choice of Letters by Entertaining Hands, 6s. 6d. net. THE SECOND POST, 6s. net. HER INFINITE VARIETY: A Feminine Portrait Gallery, 6s. net. GOOD COMPANY: A Rally of Men, 6s. net. ONE DAY AND ANOTHER, 6s. net. OLD LAMPS FOR NEW, 6s. net. LOITERER'S HARVEST, 6s. net. CLOUD AND SILVER, 6s. net. A BOSWELL OF BAGHDAD, AND OTHER ESSAYS, 6s. net. 'TWIXT EAGLE AND DOVE, 6s. net. THE PHANTOM JOURNAL, AND OTHER ESSAYS AND DIVERSIONS, 6s. net. SPECIALLY SELECTED: A Choice of Essays, 7s. 6d. net. URBANITIES. Illustrated by G. L. STAMPA, 7s. 6d. net. GIVING AND RECEIVING. 6s. net. YOU KNOW WHAT PEOPLE ARE. 5s. net. THE BRITISH SCHOOL: An Anecdotal Guide to the British Painters and Paintings in the National Gallery, 6s. net. ROVING EAST AND ROVING WEST: Notes gathered in India, Japan, and America. 5s. net. EDWIN AUSTIN ABBEY, R.A. 2 vols. £6 6s. net. VERMEER OF DELFT, 10s. 6d. net.
Masefield (John). ON THE SPANISH MAIN. A new edition. *Cr. 8vo. 8s. 6d. net.*
A SAILOR'S GARLAND. *Second Edition. Cr. 8vo. 6s. net.*
SEA LIFE IN NELSON'S TIME. Illustrated. *Second Edition. Cr. 8vo. 5s. net.*
Meldrum (D. S.). REMBRANDT'S PAINTINGS. *Wide Royal 8vo. £3 3s. net.*

Methuen (A.). AN ANTHOLOGY OF MODERN VERSE. With Introduction by ROBERT LYND. *Twelfth Edition. Fcap. 8vo. 6s. net.* Thin paper, leather, 7s. 6d. net.
SHAKESPEARE TO HARDY: AN ANTHOLOGY OF ENGLISH LYRICS. With an Introduction by ROBERT LYND. *Third Edition. Fcap. 8vo, 6s. net.* Leather, 7s. 6d. net.
McDougall (William). AN INTRODUCTION TO SOCIAL PSYCHOLOGY. *Eighteenth Edition. Cr. 8vo. 8s. 6d. net.*
BODY AND MIND: A HISTORY AND A DEFENCE OF ANIMISM. *Fifth Edition. Demy 8vo. 12s. 6d. net.*
NATIONAL WELFARE AND NATIONAL DECAY. *Cr. 8vo. 6s. net.*
Maeterlinck (Maurice)—
THE BLUE BIRD: A Fairy Play in Six Acts 6s. net. MARY MAGDALENE: A Play in Three Acts, 5s. net. DEATH, 3s. 6d. net. OUR ETERNITY, 6s. net. THE UNKNOWN GUEST, 6s. net. POEMS, 5s. net. THE WRACK OF THE STORM, 6s. net. THE MIRACLE OF ST. ANTHONY: A Play in One Act, 3s. 6d. net. THE BURGOMASTER OF STILEMONDE: A Play in Three Acts, 5s. net. THE BETROTHAL; or, The Blue Bird Chooses, 6s. net. MOUNTAIN PATHS, 6s. net. THE STORY OF TYLTYL, 21s. net. THE GREAT SECRET. 7s. 6d. net.
Milne (A. A.)—
NOT THAT IT MATTERS. *Fcap. 8vo. 6s. net.* IF I MAY. *Fcap. 8vo. 6s. net.*
Newman (Tom). HOW TO PLAY BILLIARDS. Illustrated. *Cr. 8vo. 8s. 6d. net.*
Oxenham (John)—
BEES IN AMBER; A Little Book of Thoughtful Verse. *Small Pott 8vo. Stiff Boards. 2s. net.* ALL'S WELL; A Collection of War Poems. THE KING'S HIGH WAY. THE VISION SPLENDID. THE FIERY CROSS. HIGH ALTARS: The Record of a Visit to the Battlefields of France and Flanders. HEARTS COURAGEOUS. ALL CLEAR! *All Small Pott 8vo. Paper, 1s. 3d. net; cloth boards, 2s. net.* WINDS OF THE DAWN. GENTLEMEN—THE KING, 2s. net.
Petrie (W. M. Flinders). A HISTORY OF EGYPT. Illustrated. *Six Volumes. Cr. 8vo. Each 9s. net.*
VOL. I. FROM THE IST TO THE XVITH DYNASTY. *Tenth Edition.* (12s. net.)
VOL. II. THE XVIITH AND XVIIITH DYNASTIES. *Sixth Edition.*
VOL. III. XIXTH TO XXXTH DYNASTIES. *Second Edition.*
VOL. IV. EGYPT UNDER THE PTOLEMAIC DYNASTY. J. P. MAHAFFY. *Second Edition.*
VOL. V. EGYPT UNDER ROMAN RULE. J. G. MILNE. *Second Edition.*
VOL. VI. EGYPT IN THE MIDDLE AGES STANLEY LANE POOLE. *Second Edition*

SYRIA AND EGYPT, FROM THE TELL EL AMARNA LETTERS. *Cr. 8vo.* 5s. *net.*

EGYPTIAN TALES. Translated from the Papyri. First Series, ivth to xiith Dynasty. Illustrated. *Third Edition. Cr. 8vo.* 5s. *net.*

EGYPTIAN TALES. Translated from the Papyri. Second Series, xviiith to xixth Dynasty. Illustrated. *Second Edition. Cr. 8vo.* 5s. *net.*

Pollitt (Arthur W.). THE ENJOYMENT OF MUSIC. *Second Edition. Cr. 8vo.* 5s. *net.*

Price (L. L.). A SHORT HISTORY OF POLITICAL ECONOMY IN ENGLAND FROM ADAM SMITH TO ARNOLD TOYNBEE. *Eleventh Edition. Cr. 8vo.* 5s. *net.*

Selous (Edmund)—
TOMMY SMITH'S ANIMALS. TOMMY SMITH'S OTHER ANIMALS. TOMMY SMITH AT THE ZOO. TOMMY SMITH AGAIN AT THE ZOO. *Each* 2s. 9d. JACK'S INSECTS, 3s. 6d. JACK'S OTHER INSECTS, 3s. 6d.

Shelley (Percy Bysshe). POEMS. With an Introduction by A. CLUTTON-BROCK and Notes by C. D. LOCOCK. *Two Volumes. Demy 8vo.* £1 1s. *net.*

SHELLEY: THE MAN AND THE POET. By A. CLUTTON-BROCK. *Fcap 8vo.* 7s. 6s. *net.*

Smith (Adam). THE WEALTH OF NATIONS. Edited by EDWIN CANNAN. *Two Volumes. Third Edition. Demy 8vo.* £1 5s. *net.*

Smith (S. C. Kaines). LOOKING AT PICTURES. Illustrated. *Second Edition. Fcap. 8vo.* 6s. *net.*

Sommerfeld (Prof. Arnold). ATOMIC STRUCTURE AND SPECTRAL LINES. *Demy 8vo.* 32s. *net.*

Stevenson (R. L.). THE LETTERS OF ROBERT LOUIS STEVENSON. Edited by SIR SIDNEY COLVIN. *A New Rearranged Edition in four volumes. Fourth Edition. Fcap. 8vo. Each* 6s. *net.*

Surtees (R. S.)—
HANDLEY CROSS, 7s. 6d. *net.* MR. SPONGE'S SPORTING TOUR, 7s. 6d. *net.* ASK MAMMA: or, The Richest Commoner in England, 7s. 6d. *net.* JORROCKS'S JAUNTS AND JOLLITIES, 6s. *net.* MR. FACEY ROMFORD'S HOUNDS, 7s. 6d. *net.* HAWBUCK GRANGE; or, The Sporting Adventures of Thomas Scott, Esq., 6s. *net.* PLAIN OR RINGLETS? 7s. 6d. *net.* HILLINGDON HALL, 7s. 6d. *net.*

Tilden (W. T.). THE ART OF LAWN TENNIS. Illustrated. *Fifth Edition. Cr. 8vo.* 6s. *net.*

Tileston (Mary W.). DAILY STRENGTH FOR DAILY NEEDS. *Twenty-eighth Edition. Medium 16mo.* 3s. 6d. *net.*

Underhill (Evelyn). MYSTICISM. A Study in the Nature and Development of Man's Spiritual Consciousness. *Ninth Edition. Demy 8vo.* 15s. *net.*

THE LIFE OF THE SPIRIT AND THE LIFE OF TO-DAY. *Cr. 8vo.* 8s. 6d. *net.*

Vardon (Harry). HOW TO PLAY GOLF. Illustrated. *Sixteenth Edition. Cr. 8vo.* 5s. 6d. *net.*

Wade (G. W.). NEW TESTAMENT HISTORY. *Demy 8vo.* 18s. *net.*

OLD TESTAMENT HISTORY. *Ninth Edition. Cr. 8vo.* 7s. 6d. *net.*

Waterhouse (Elizabeth). A LITTLE BOOK OF LIFE AND DEATH. *Twenty-first Edition. Small Pott 8vo.* 2s. 6d. *net.*

Wells (J.). A SHORT HISTORY OF ROME. *Eighteenth Edition.* With 3 Maps. *Cr. 8vo.* 5s.

Wilde (Oscar). THE WORKS OF OSCAR WILDE. *Fcap. 8vo. Each* 6s. 6d. *net.*
I. LORD ARTHUR SAVILE'S CRIME AND THE PORTRAIT OF MR. W. H. II. THE DUCHESS OF PADUA. III. POEMS. IV. LADY WINDERMERE'S FAN. V. A WOMAN OF NO IMPORTANCE. VI. AN IDEAL HUSBAND. VII. THE IMPORTANCE OF BEING EARNEST. VIII. A HOUSE OF POMEGRANATES. IX. INTENTIONS. X. DE PROFUNDIS AND PRISON LETTERS. XI. ESSAYS. XII. SALOME, A FLORENTINE TRAGEDY, and LA SAINTE COURTISANE. XIII. A CRITIC IN PALL MALL. XIV. SELECTED PROSE OF OSCAR WILDE. XV. ART AND DECORATION.

FOR LOVE OF THE KING. A BURMESE MASQUE. *Demy 8vo.* 8s. 6d. *net.*

Yeats (W. B.). A BOOK OF IRISH VERSE. *Fourth Edition. Cr. 8vo.* 7s. *net.*

PART II.—A SELECTION OF SERIES
The Antiquary's Books
Demy 8vo. 10s. 6d. *net each volume. With Numerous Illustrations.*

ANCIENT PAINTED GLASS IN ENGLAND. ARCHÆOLOGY AND FALSE ANTIQUITIES. THE BELLS OF ENGLAND. THE BRASSES OF ENGLAND. THE CASTLES AND WALLED TOWNS OF ENGLAND. CELTIC ART IN PAGAN AND CHRISTIAN TIMES. CHURCHWARDENS' ACCOUNTS. THE DOMESDAY INQUEST. ENGLISH CHURCH FURNITURE. ENGLISH COSTUME. ENGLISH MONASTIC LIFE. ENGLISH SEALS. FOLK-LORE AS AN HISTORICAL SCIENCE. THE GUILDS AND COMPANIES OF LONDON. THE HERMITS AND ANCHORITES OF ENGLAND. THE MANOR AND MANORIAL RECORDS. THE MEDIÆVAL HOSPITALS OF ENGLAND. OLD ENGLISH INSTRUMENTS OF MUSIC. OLD ENGLISH LIBRARIES. OLD SERVICE BOOKS OF THE ENGLISH CHURCH. PARISH LIFE IN MEDIÆVAL ENGLAND. THE PARISH REGISTERS OF ENGLAND. REMAINS OF THE PREHISTORIC AGE IN ENGLAND. THE ROMAN ERA IN BRITAIN. ROMANO-BRITISH BUILDINGS AND EARTHWORKS. THE ROYAL FORESTS OF ENGLAND. THE SCHOOLS OF MEDIÆVAL ENGLAND. SHRINES OF BRITISH SAINTS.

The Arden Shakespeare
General Editor, R. H. CASE
Demy 8vo. 6s. net each volume

An edition of Shakespeare in Single Plays; each edited with a full Introduction, Textual Notes, and a Commentary at the foot of the page.

The Arden Shakespeare will be completed shortly by the publication of THE SECOND PART OF KING HENRY IV. Edited by R. P. COWL. MUCH ADO ABOUT NOTHING. Edited by GRACE TRENERY.

Classics of Art
Edited by DR. J. H. W. LAING
With numerous Illustrations. Wide Royal 8vo

THE ART OF THE GREEKS, 21s. net. THE ART OF THE ROMANS, 16s. net. CHARDIN, 15s. net. DONATELLO, 16s. net. GEORGE ROMNEY, 15s. net. GHIRLANDAIO, 15s. net. LAWRENCE, 25s. net. MICHELANGELO, 15s. net. RAPHAEL, 15s. net. REMBRANDT'S ETCHINGS, 31s. 6d. net. REMBRANDT'S PAINTINGS, 63s. net. RUBENS, 30s. net. TINTORETTO, 16s. net. TITIAN, 16s. net. TURNER'S SKETCHES AND DRAWINGS, 15s. net. VELASQUEZ, 15s. net.

The 'Complete' Series
Fully Illustrated. Demy 8vo

THE COMPLETE AIRMAN, 16s. net. THE COMPLETE AMATEUR BOXER, 10s. 6d. net. THE COMPLETE ASSOCIATION FOOTBALLER, 10s. 6d. net. THE COMPLETE ATHLETIC TRAINER, 10s. 6d. net. THE COMPLETE BILLIARD PLAYER, 10s. 6d. net. THE COMPLETE COOK, 10s. 6d. net. THE COMPLETE FOXHUNTER, 16s. net. THE COMPLETE GOLFER, 12s. 6d. net. THE COMPLETE HOCKEY PLAYER, 10s. 6d. net. THE COMPLETE HORSEMAN, 15s. net. THE COMPLETE JUJITSUAN. *Cr. 8vo.* 5s. net. THE COMPLETE LAWN TENNIS PLAYER, 12s. 6d. net. THE COMPLETE MOTORIST, 10s. 6d. net. THE COMPLETE MOUNTAINEER, 18s. net. THE COMPLETE OARSMAN, 15s. net. THE COMPLETE PHOTOGRAPHER, 12s. 6d. net. THE COMPLETE RUGBY FOOTBALLER, ON THE NEW ZEALAND SYSTEM, 12s. 6d. net. THE COMPLETE SHOT, 16s. net. THE COMPLETE SWIMMER, 10s. 6d. net. THE COMPLETE YACHTSMAN, 18s. net.

The Connoisseur's Library
With numerous Illustrations. Wide Royal 8vo. £1 11s. 6d. net each volume

ENGLISH COLOURED BOOKS. ETCHINGS. EUROPEAN ENAMELS. FINE BOOKS. GLASS. GOLDSMITHS' AND SILVERSMITHS' WORK. ILLUMINATED MANUSCRIPTS. IVORIES. JEWELLERY. MEZZOTINTS. MINIATURES. PORCELAIN. SEALS. WOOD SCULPTURE.

Handbooks of Theology
Demy 8vo

THE DOCTRINE OF THE INCARNATION, 15s. net. A HISTORY OF EARLY CHRISTIAN DOCTRINE, 16s. net. INTRODUCTION TO THE HISTORY OF RELIGION, 12s. 6d. net. AN INTRODUCTION TO THE HISTORY OF THE CREEDS, 12s. 6d. net. THE PHILOSOPHY OF RELIGION IN ENGLAND AND AMERICA, 12s. 6d. net. THE XXXIX ARTICLES OF THE CHURCH OF ENGLAND, 15s. net.

Health Series
Fcap. 8vo. 2s. 6d. net

THE BABY. THE CARE OF THE BODY. THE CARE OF THE TEETH. THE EYES OF OUR CHILDREN. HEALTH FOR THE MIDDLE-AGED. THE HEALTH OF A WOMAN. THE HEALTH OF THE SKIN. HOW TO LIVE LONG. THE PREVENTION OF THE COMMON COLD. STAYING THE PLAGUE. THROAT AND EAR TROUBLES. TUBERCULOSIS. THE HEALTH OF THE CHILD, 2s. net.

The Library of Devotion

Handy Editions of the great Devotional Books, well edited
With Introductions and (where necessary) Notes
Small Pott 8vo, cloth, 3s. net and 3s. 6d. net

Little Books on Art

With many Illustrations. Demy 16mo. 5s. net each volume

Each volume consists of about 200 pages, and contains from 30 to 40 Illustrations, including a Frontispiece in Photogravure

ALBRECHT DÜRER. THE ARTS OF JAPAN. BOOKPLATES. BOTTICELLI. BURNE-JONES. CELLINI. CHRISTIAN SYMBOLISM. CHRIST IN ART. CLAUDE. CONSTABLE. COROT. EARLY ENGLISH WATER-COLOUR. ENAMELS. FREDERIC LEIGHTON. GEORGE ROMNEY. GREEK ART. GREUZE AND BOUCHER. HOLBEIN. ILLUMINATED MANUSCRIPTS. JEWELLERY. JOHN HOPPNER. SIR JOSHUA REYNOLDS. MILLET. MINIATURES. OUR LADY IN ART. RAPHAEL. RODIN. TURNER. VANDYCK. WATTS.

The Little Guides

With many Illustrations by E. H. NEW and other artists, and from photographs

Small Pott 8vo. 4s. net to 7s. 6d. net.

Guides to the English and Welsh Counties, and some well-known districts

The main features of these Guides are (1) a handy and charming form; (2) illustrations from photographs and by well-known artists; (3) good plans and maps; (4) an adequate but compact presentation of everything that is interesting in the natural features, history, archæology, and architecture of the town or district treated.

The Little Quarto Shakespeare

Edited by W. J. CRAIG. With Introductions and Notes
*Pott 16mo. 40 Volumes. Leather, price 1s. 9d. net each volume
Cloth, 1s. 6d. net.*

Plays

Fcap. 8vo. 3s. 6d. net

MILESTONES. Arnold Bennett and Edward Knoblock. *Eleventh Edition.*
IDEAL HUSBAND, AN. Oscar Wilde. *Acting Edition.*
KISMET. Edward Knoblock. *Fourth Edition.*
THE GREAT ADVENTURE. Arnold Bennett. *Fifth Edition.*
TYPHOON. A Play in Four Acts. Melchior Lengyel. English Version by Laurence Irving. *Second Edition.*
WARE CASE, THE. George Pleydell.
GENERAL POST. J. E. Harold Terry. *Second Edition.*
THE HONEYMOON. Arnold Bennett. *Third Edition.*

MESSRS. METHUEN'S PUBLICATIONS 7

Sports Series
Illustrated. Fcap. 8vo

All About Flying, 3s. net. Alpine Ski-ing at All Heights and Seasons, 5s. net. Cross Country Ski-ing, 5s. net. Golf Do's and Dont's, 2s. 6d. net. Quick Cuts to Good Golf, 2s. 6d. net. Inspired Golf, 2s. 6d. net. Driving, Approaching, Putting, 2s. net. Golf Clubs and How to Use Them, 2s. net. The Secret of Golf for Occasional Players, 2s. net. Lawn Tennis, 3s. net. Lawn Tennis Do's and Dont's, 2s. net. Lawn Tennis for Young Players, 2s. 6d. net. Lawn Tennis for Club Players, 2s. 6d. net. Lawn Tennis for Match Players, 2s. 6d. net. Hockey, 4s. net. How to Swim, 2s. net. Punting, 3s. 6d. net. Skating, 3s. net. Wrestling, 2s. net.

The Westminster Commentaries
General Editor, WALTER LOCK
Demy 8vo

The Acts of the Apostles, 12s. 6d. net. Amos, 8s. 6d. net. I Corinthians, 8s. 6d. net. Exodus, 15s. net. Ezekiel, 12s. 6d. net. Genesis, 16s. net. Hebrews, 8s. 6d. net. Isaiah, 16s. net. Jeremiah, 16s. net. Job, 8s. 6d. net. The Pastoral Epistles, 8s. 6d. net. The Philippians, 8s. 6d. net. St. James, 8s. 6d. net. St. Matthew, 15s. net. St. Luke, 15s. net.

Methuen's Two-Shilling Library
Cheap Editions of many Popular Books
Fcap. 8vo

PART III.—A Selection of Works of Fiction

Bennett (Arnold)—
Clayhanger, 8s. net. Hilda Lessways, 8s. 6d. net. These Twain. The Card. The Regent: A Five Towns Story of Adventure in London. The Price of Love. Buried Alive. A Man from the North. Whom God hath Joined. A Great Man: A Frolic. Mr. Prohack. All 7s. 6d. net. The Matador of the Five Towns, 6s. net.

Birmingham (George A.)—
Spanish Gold. The Search Party. Lalage's Lovers. The Bad Times. Up, the Rebels. The Lost Lawyer. All 7s. 6d. net. Inisheeny, 8s. 6d. net. The Great-Grandmother, 7s. 6d. net. Found Money, 7s. 6d. net.

Burroughs (Edgar Rice)—
Tarzan of the Apes, 6s. net. The Return of Tarzan, 6s. net. The Beasts of Tarzan, 6s. net. The Son of Tarzan, 6s. net. Jungle Tales of Tarzan, 6s. net. Tarzan and the Jewels of Opar, 6s. net. Tarzan the Untamed, 7s. 6d. net. A Princess of Mars, 6s. net. The Gods of Mars, 6s. net. The Warlord of Mars, 6s. net. Thuvia, Maid of Mars, 6s. net. Tarzan the Terrible, 2s. 6d. net. The Mucker, 6s. net. The Man without a Soul, 6s. net. The Chessmen of Mars, 6s. net. At the Earth's Core, 6s. net.

Conrad (Joseph)—
A Set of Six, 7s. 6d. net. Victory: An Island Tale. Cr. 8vo. 9s. net. The Secret Agent: A Simple Tale. Cr. 8vo. 9s. net. Under Western Eyes. Cr. 8vo. 9s. net. Chance. Cr. 8vo. 9s. net.

Corelli (Marie)—
A Romance of Two Worlds, 7s. 6d. net. Vendetta: or, The Story of One Forgotten, 8s. net. Thelma: A Norwegian Princess, 8s. 6d. net. Ardath: The Story of a Dead Self, 7s. 6d. net. The Soul of Lilith, 7s. 6d. net. Wormwood: A Drama of Paris. 8s. net. Barabbas: A Dream of the World's Tragedy, 7s. 6d. net. The Sorrows of Satan, 7s. 6d. net. The Master-Christian, 8s. 6d. net. Temporal Power: A Study in Supremacy, 6s. net. God's Good Man: A Simple Love Story, 8s. 6d. net. Holy Orders: The Tragedy of a Quiet Life, 8s. 6d. net. The Mighty Atom, 7s. 6d. net. Boy: A Sketch, 7s. 6d. net. Cameos, 6s. net. The Life Everlasting, 8s. 6d. net. The Love of Long Ago, and Other Stories, 8s. 6d. net. Innocent, 7s. 6d. net. The Secret Power: A Romance of the Time, 6s. net.

Hichens (Robert)—
Tongues of Conscience, 7s. 6d. net. Felix: Three Years in a Life, 7s. 6d. net. The Woman with the Fan, 7s. 6d. net. The Garden of Allah, 8s. 6d. net. The Call of the Blood, 8s. 6d. net. The Dweller on the Threshold, 7s. 6d. net. The Way of Ambition, 7s. 6d. net. In the Wilderness, 7s. 6d. net.

Hope (Anthony)—
A CHANGE OF AIR. A MAN OF MARK. SIMON DALE. THE KING'S MIRROR. THE DOLLY DIALOGUES. MRS. MAXON PROTESTS. A YOUNG MAN'S YEAR. BEAUMAROY HOME FROM THE WARS. *All* 7s. 6d. *net.*

Jacobs (W. W.)—
MANY CARGOES, 5s. net. SEA URCHINS, 5s. net and 3s. 6d. net. A MASTER OF CRAFT, 6s. net. LIGHT FREIGHTS, 6s. net. THE SKIPPER'S WOOING, 5s. net. AT SUNWICH PORT, 5s. net. DIALSTONE LANE, 5s. net. ODD CRAFT, 5s. net. THE LADY OF THE BARGE, 5s. net. SALTHAVEN, 6s. net. SAILORS' KNOTS, 5s. net. SHORT CRUISES, 6s. net.

London (Jack)— WHITE FANG. Ninth Edition. *Cr.* 8vo. 7s. 6d. *net.*

Lucas (E. V.)—
LISTENER'S LURE: An Oblique Narration, 6s. net. OVER BEMERTON'S: An Easygoing Chronicle, 6s. net. MR. INGLESIDE, 6s. net. LONDON LAVENDER, 6s. net. LANDMARKS, 6s. net. THE VERMILION BOX, 6s. net. VERENA IN THE MIDST, 8s. 6d. net. ROSE AND ROSE, 6s. net. GENEVRA'S MONEY, 7s. 6d. net.

McKenna (Stephen)—
SONIA: Between Two Worlds, 8s. net. NINETY-SIX HOURS' LEAVE, 7s. 6d. net. THE SIXTH SENSE, 6s. net. MIDAS & SON, 8s. net.

Malet (Lucas)—
THE HISTORY OF SIR RICHARD CALMADY: A Romance. 10s. net. THE CARISSIMA. THE GATELESS BARRIER. DEADHAM HARD. *All* 7s. 6d. *net.* THE WAGES OF SIN. 8s. net. COLONEL ENDERBY'S WIFE, 7s. 6d. net.

Mason (A. E. W.). CLEMENTINA. Illustrated. *Ninth Edition.* 7s. 6d. *net.*

Milne (A. A.)—
THE DAY'S PLAY. THE HOLIDAY ROUND. ONCE A WEEK. *All* 7s. 6d. *net.* THE SUNNY SIDE. 6s. *net.* THE RED HOUSE MYSTERY. 6s. *net.*

Oxenham (John)—
THE QUEST OF THE GOLDEN ROSE. MARY ALL-ALONE. 7s. 6d. *net.*

Parker (Gilbert)—
MRS. FALCHION. THE TRANSLATION OF A SAVAGE. WHEN VALMOND CAME TO PONTIAC: The Story of a Lost Napoleon. AN ADVENTURE OF THE NORTH: The Last Adventures of 'Pretty Pierre.' THE SEATS OF THE MIGHTY. THE BATTLE OF THE STRONG: A Romance of Two Kingdoms. THE TRAIL OF THE SWORD. NORTHERN LIGHTS. JUDGEMENT HOUSE. *All* 7s. 6d. *net.*

Phillpotts (Eden)—
CHILDREN OF THE MIST. THE RIVER. THE HUMAN BOY AND THE WAR. *All* 7s. 6d. *net.*

Rohmer (Sax)—
THE GOLDEN SCORPION. 7s. 6d. *net.* THE DEVIL DOCTOR. THE MYSTERY OF DR. FU-MANCHU. THE YELLOW CLAW. *All* 3s. 6d. *net.*

Swinnerton (F.) SHOPS AND HOUSES. SEPTEMBER. THE HAPPY FAMILY. ON THE STAIRCASE. COQUETTE. THE CHASTE WIFE. *All* 7s. 6d. *net.* THE MERRY HEART, THE CASEMENT, THE YOUNG IDEA. *All* 6s. *net.* THE THREE LOVERS, 7s. 6d. *net.*

Wells (H. G.). BEALBY. Fourth Edition. *Cr.* 8vo. 7s. 6d. *net.*

Williamson (C. N. and A. M.)—
THE LIGHTNING CONDUCTOR: The Strange Adventures of a Motor Car. LADY BETTY ACROSS THE WATER. IT HAPPENED IN EGYPT. THE SHOP GIRL. THE LIGHTNING CONDUCTRESS. MY FRIEND THE CHAUFFEUR. SET IN SILVER. THE GREAT PEARL SECRET. THE LOVE PIRATE. *All* 7s. 6d. *net.* CRUCIFIX CORNER. 6s. *net.*

Methuen's Half-Crown Novels
Crown 8vo
Cheap Editions of many of the most Popular Novels of the day
Write for a Complete List

Methuen's Two-Shilling Novels
Fcap. 8vo
Write for Complete List

ND - #0012 - 090623 - C0 - 229/152/18 [20] - CB - 9780265188149 - Gloss Lamination